ADORABLE BABY ANIMALS

- Coloring Book -

This book belong to:

____

____

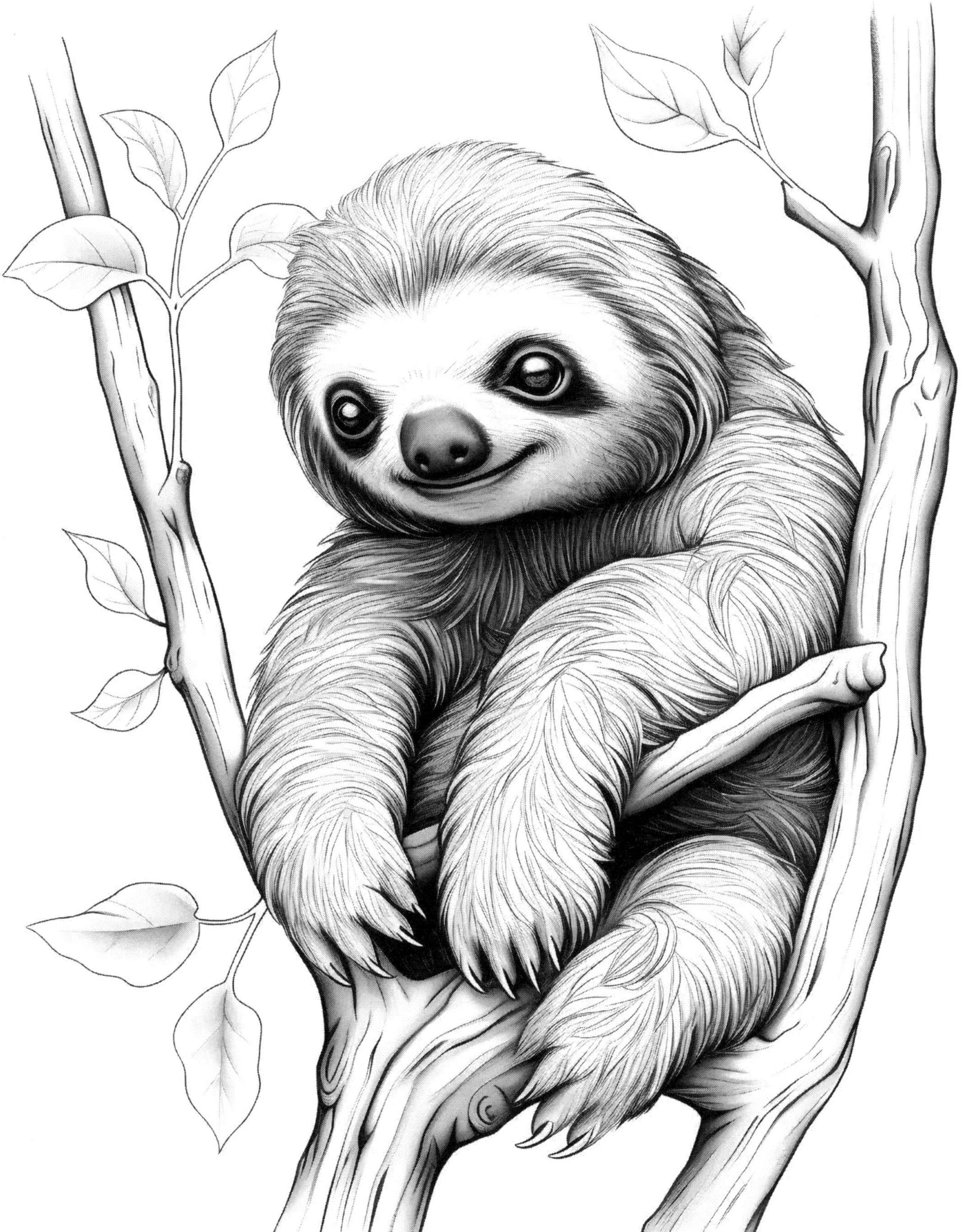

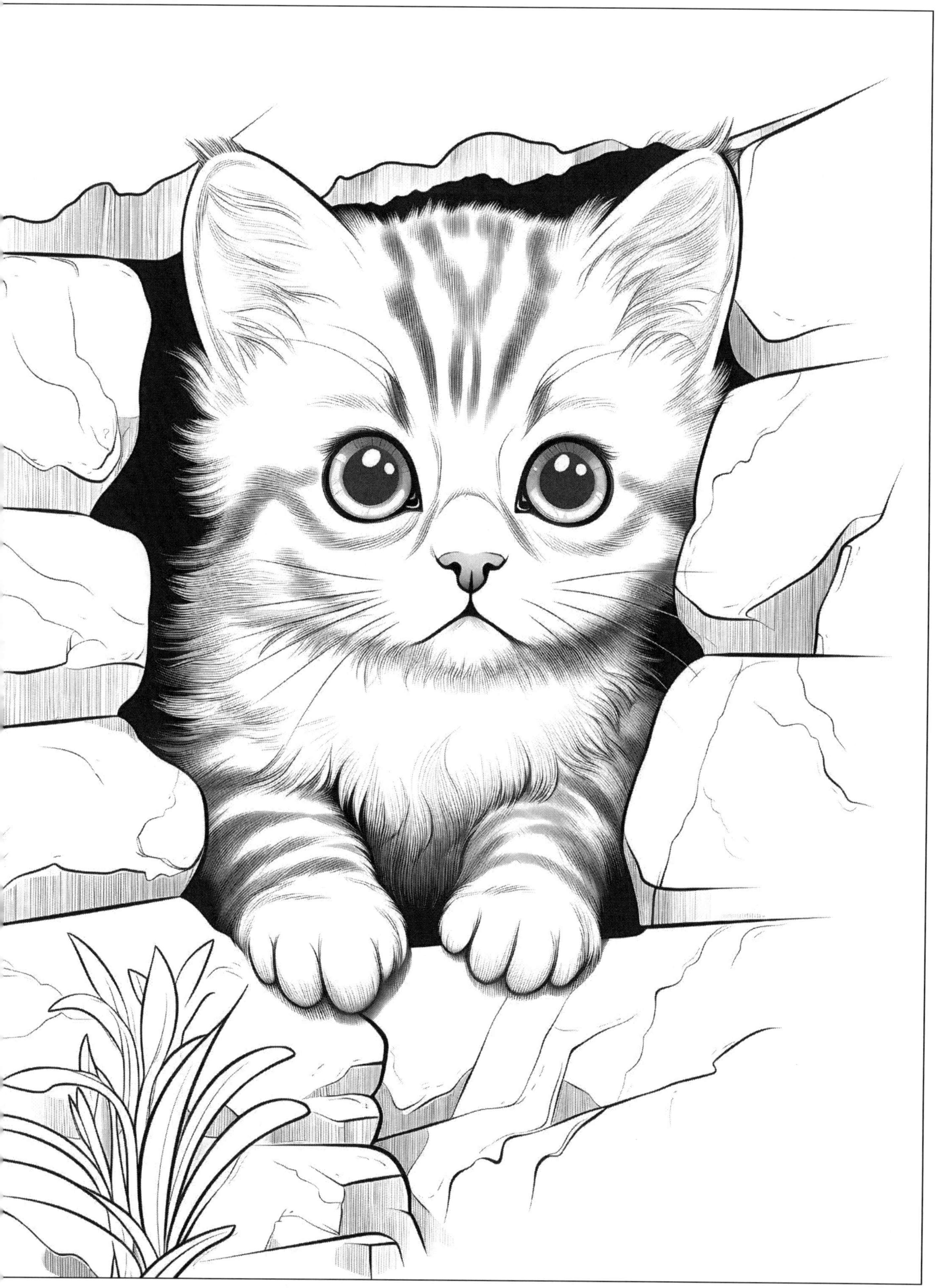

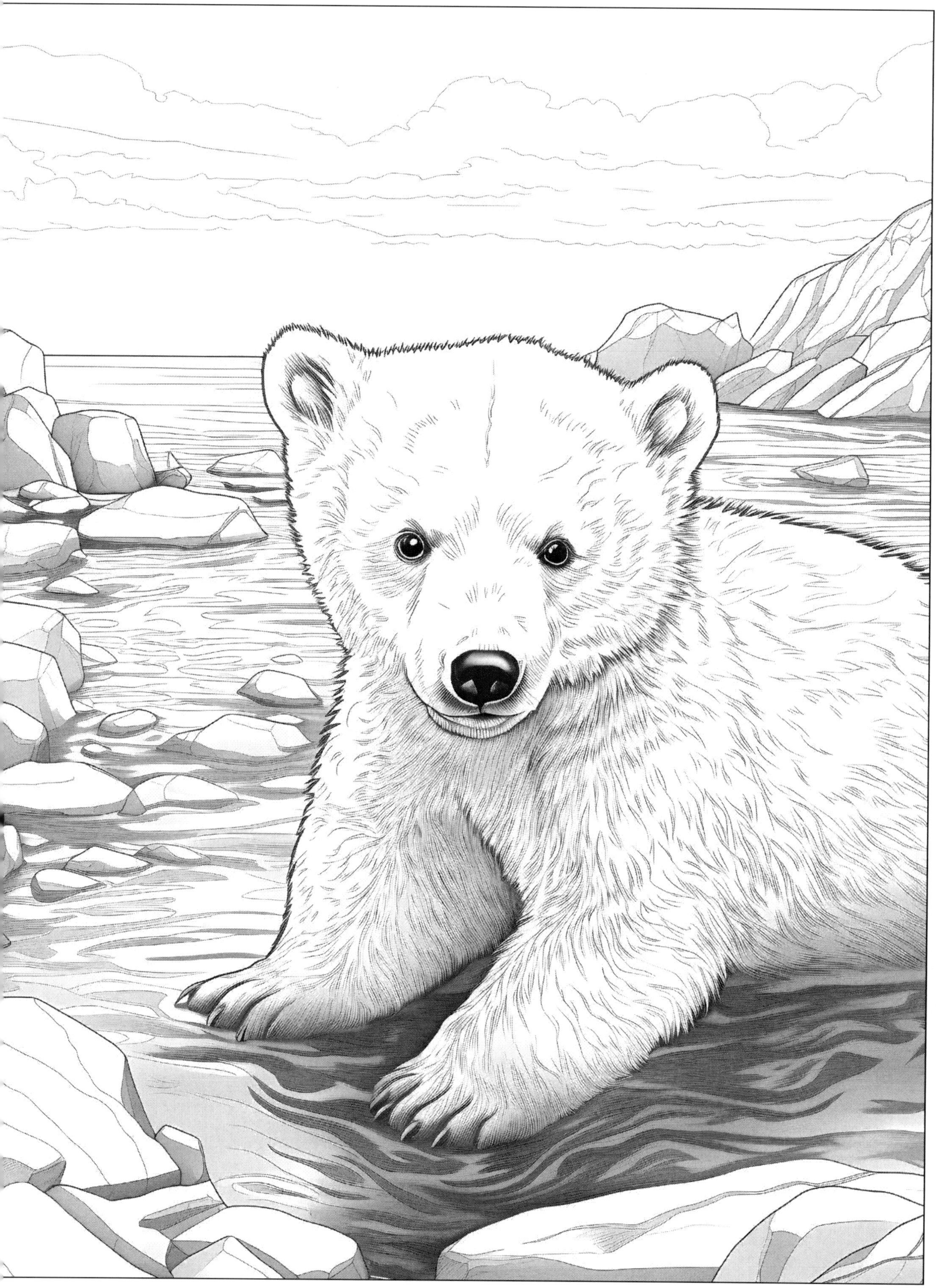

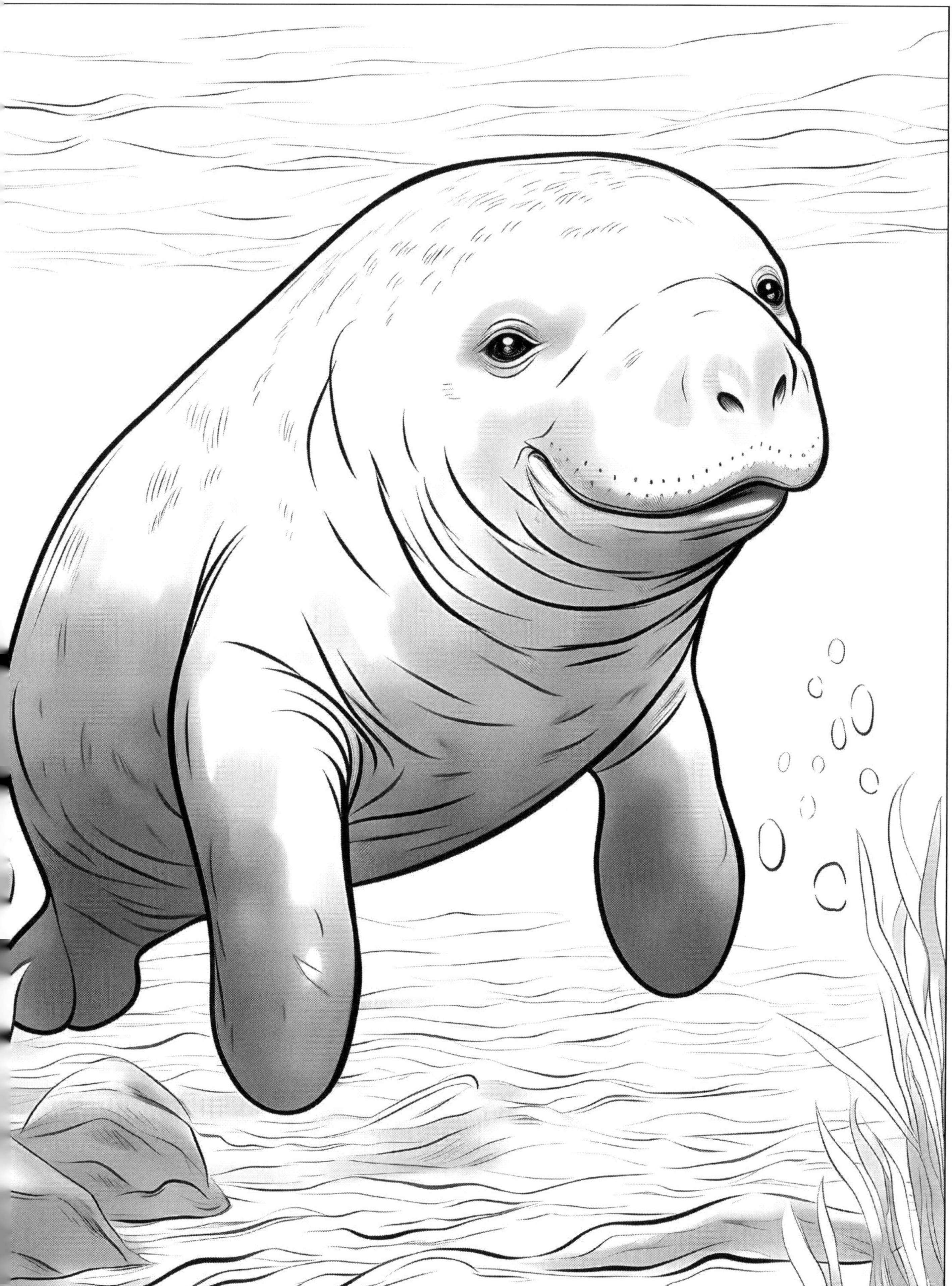

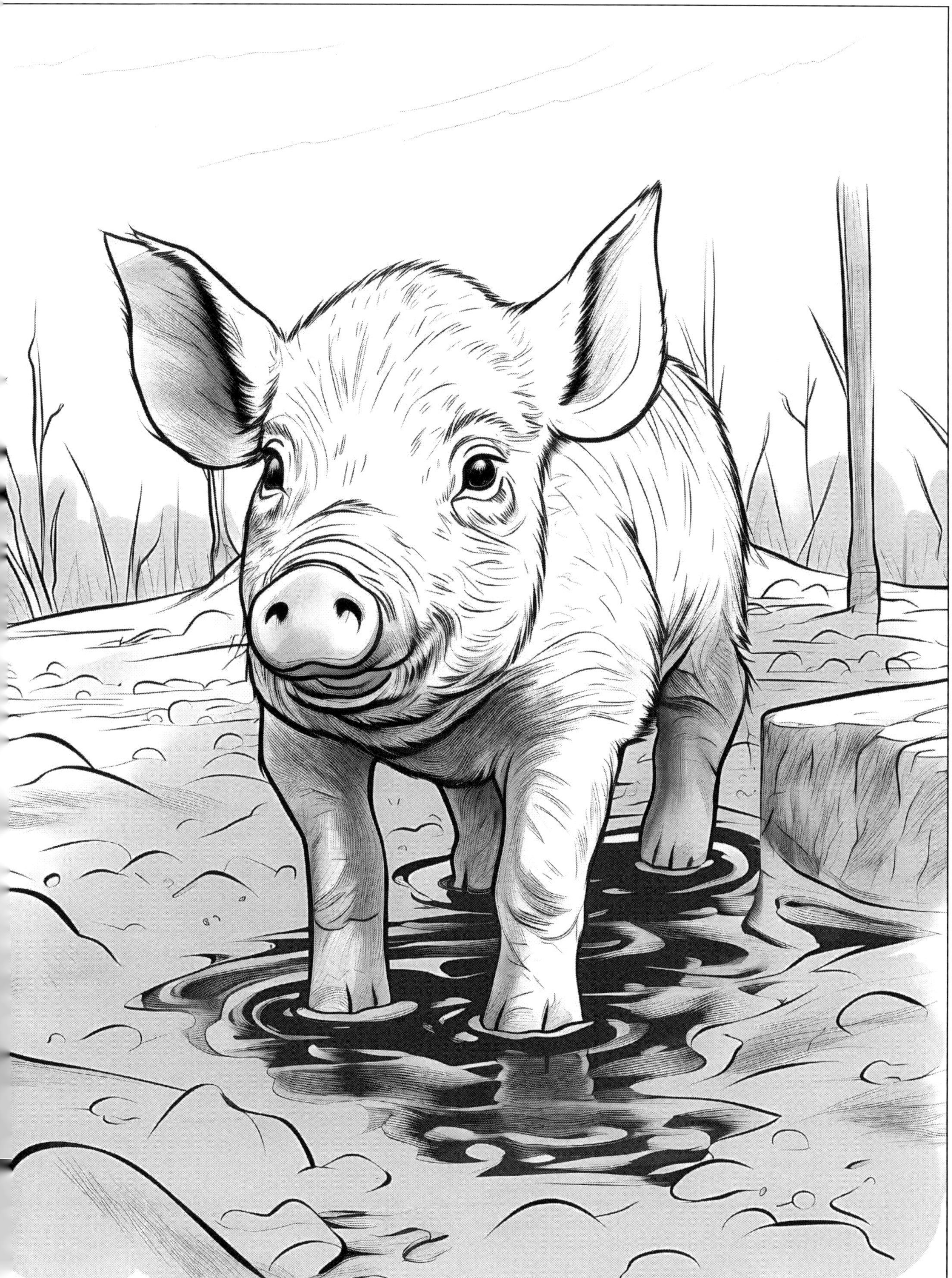

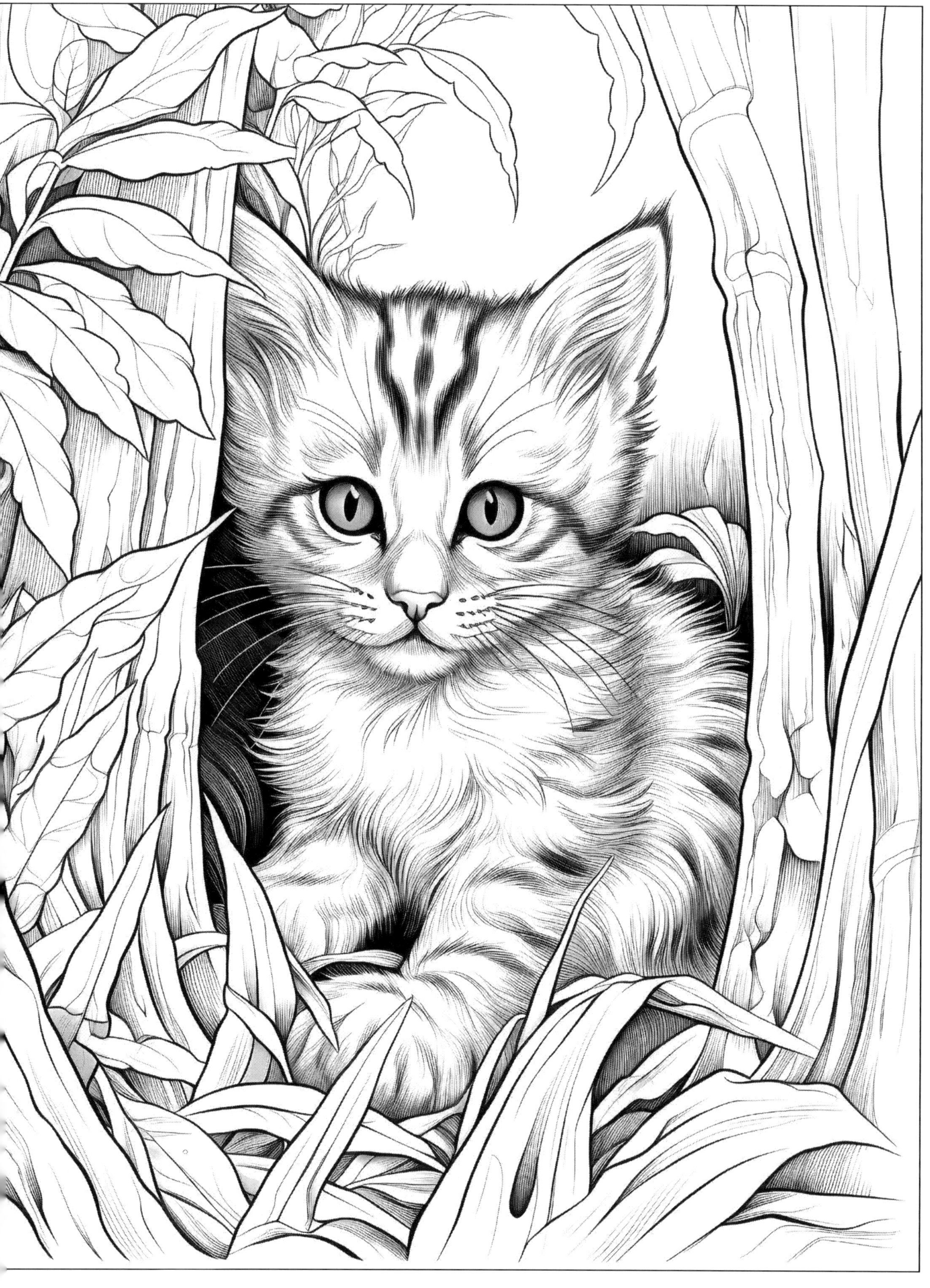

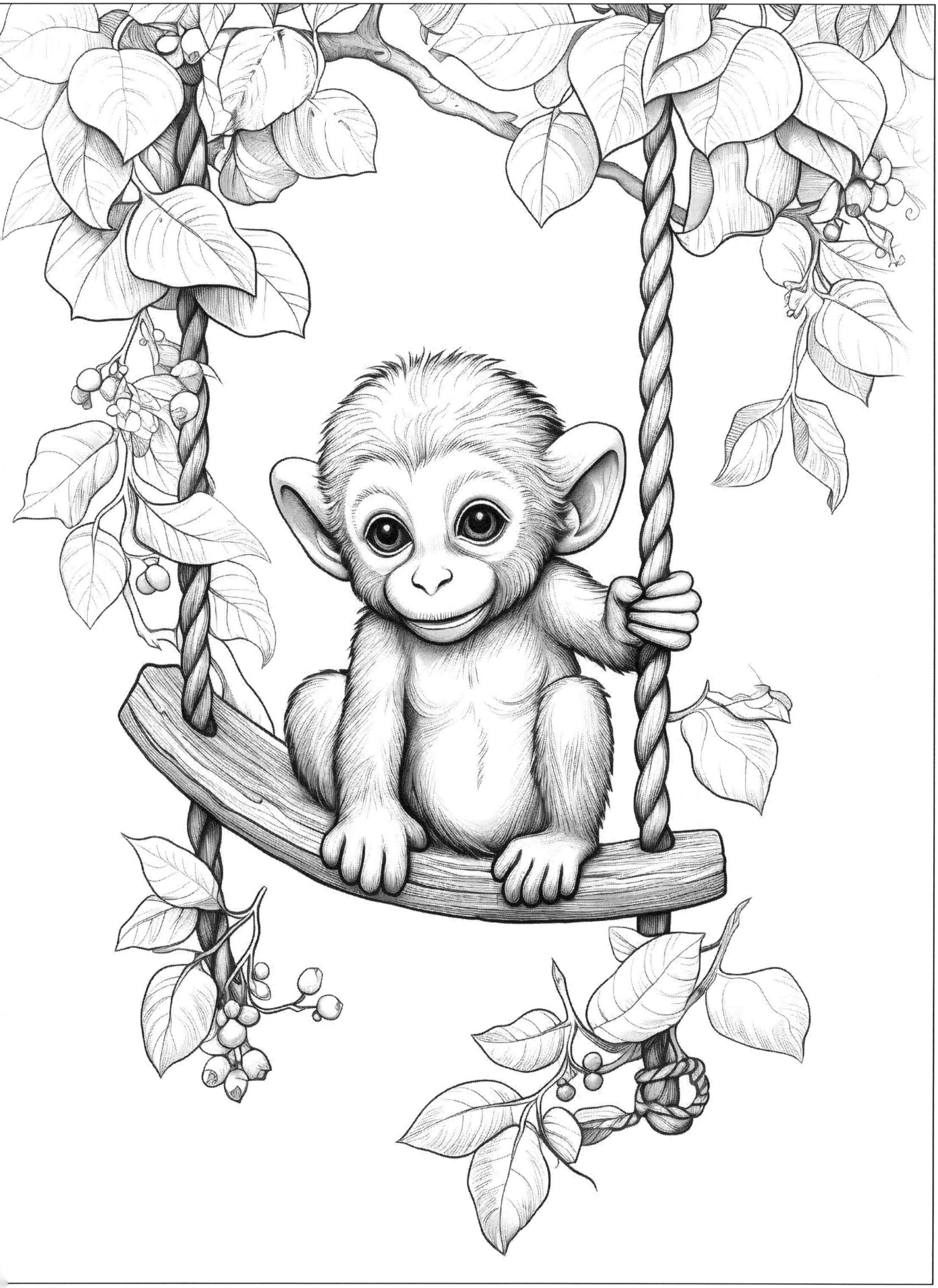

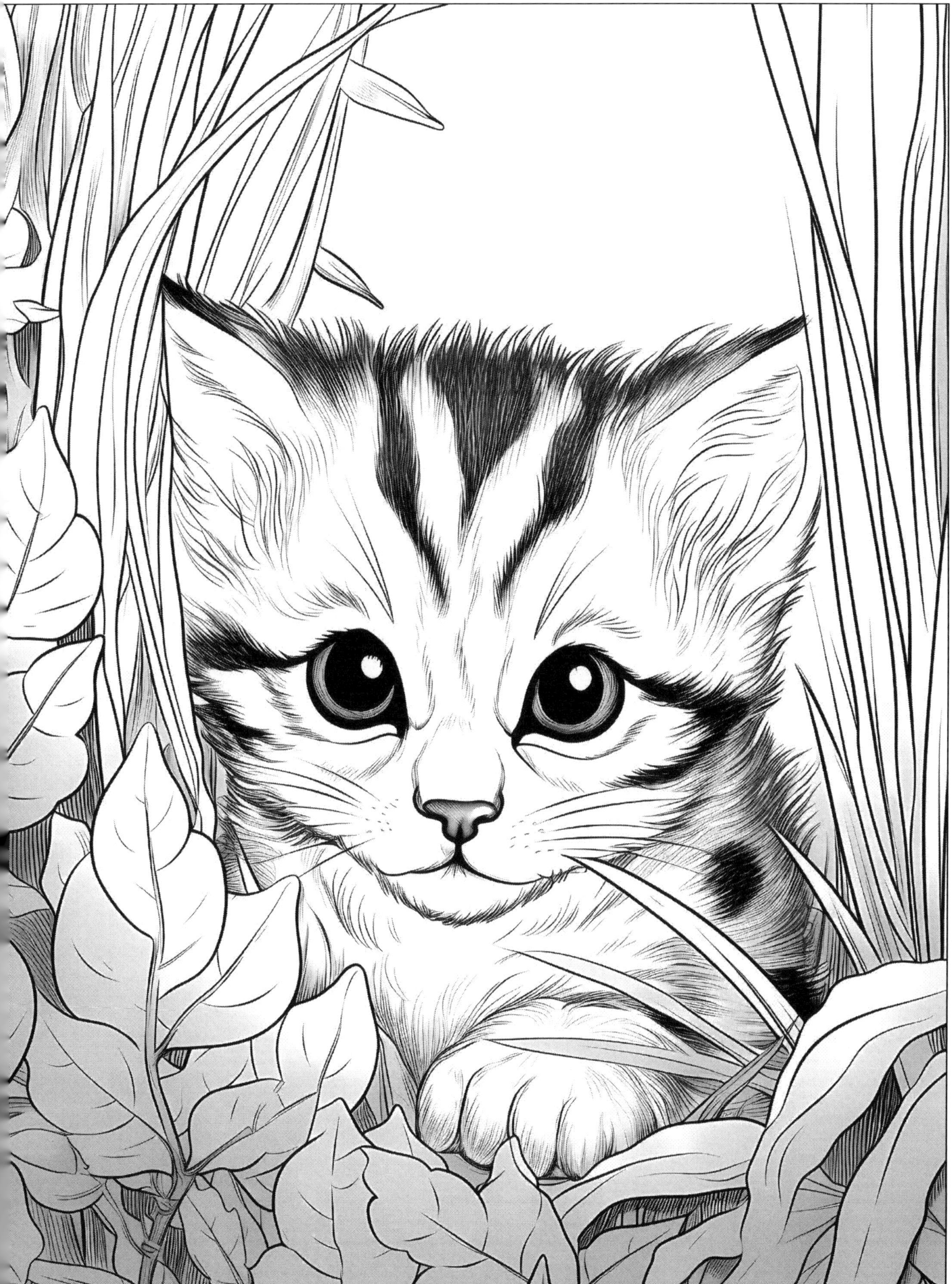

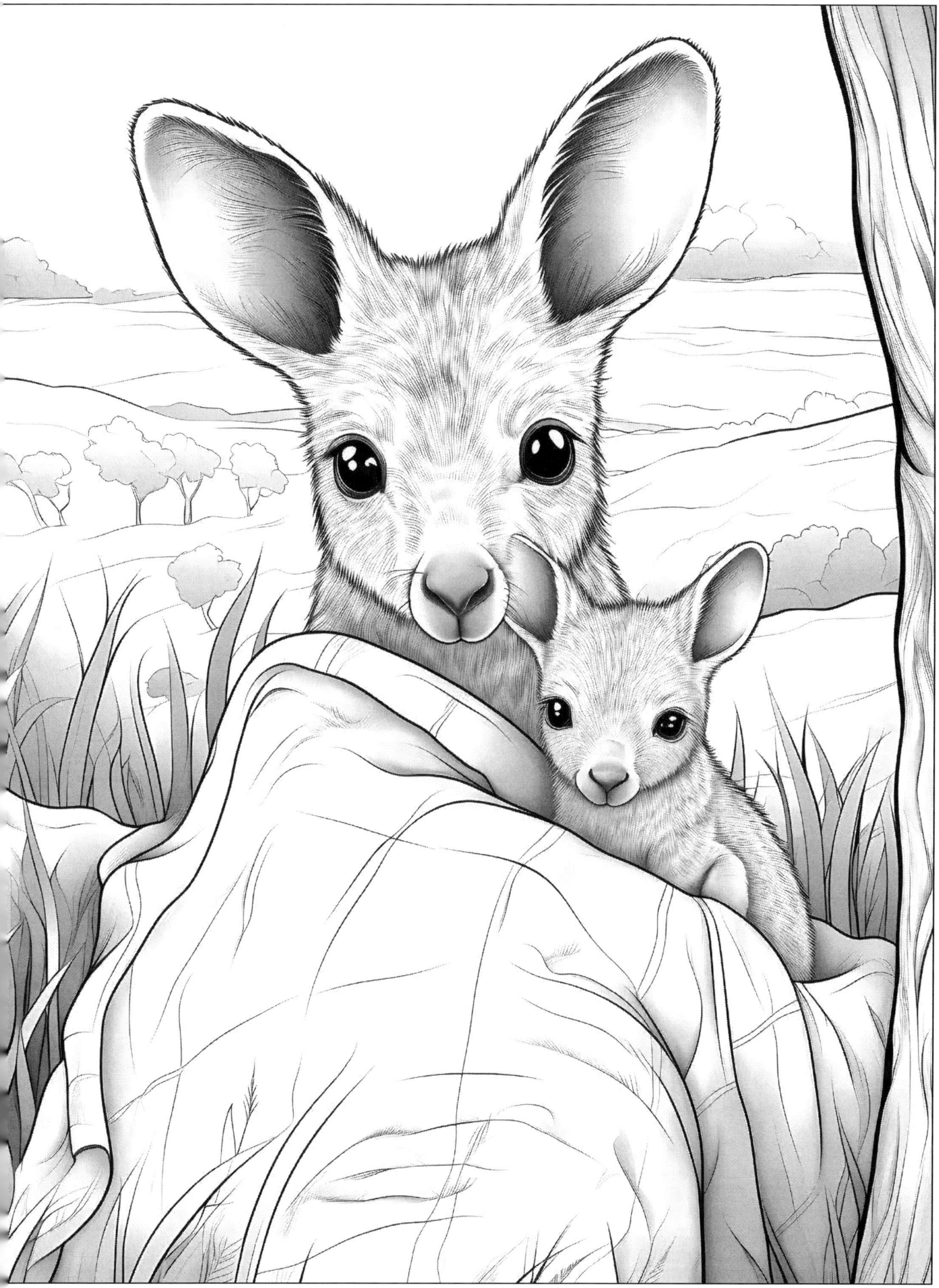

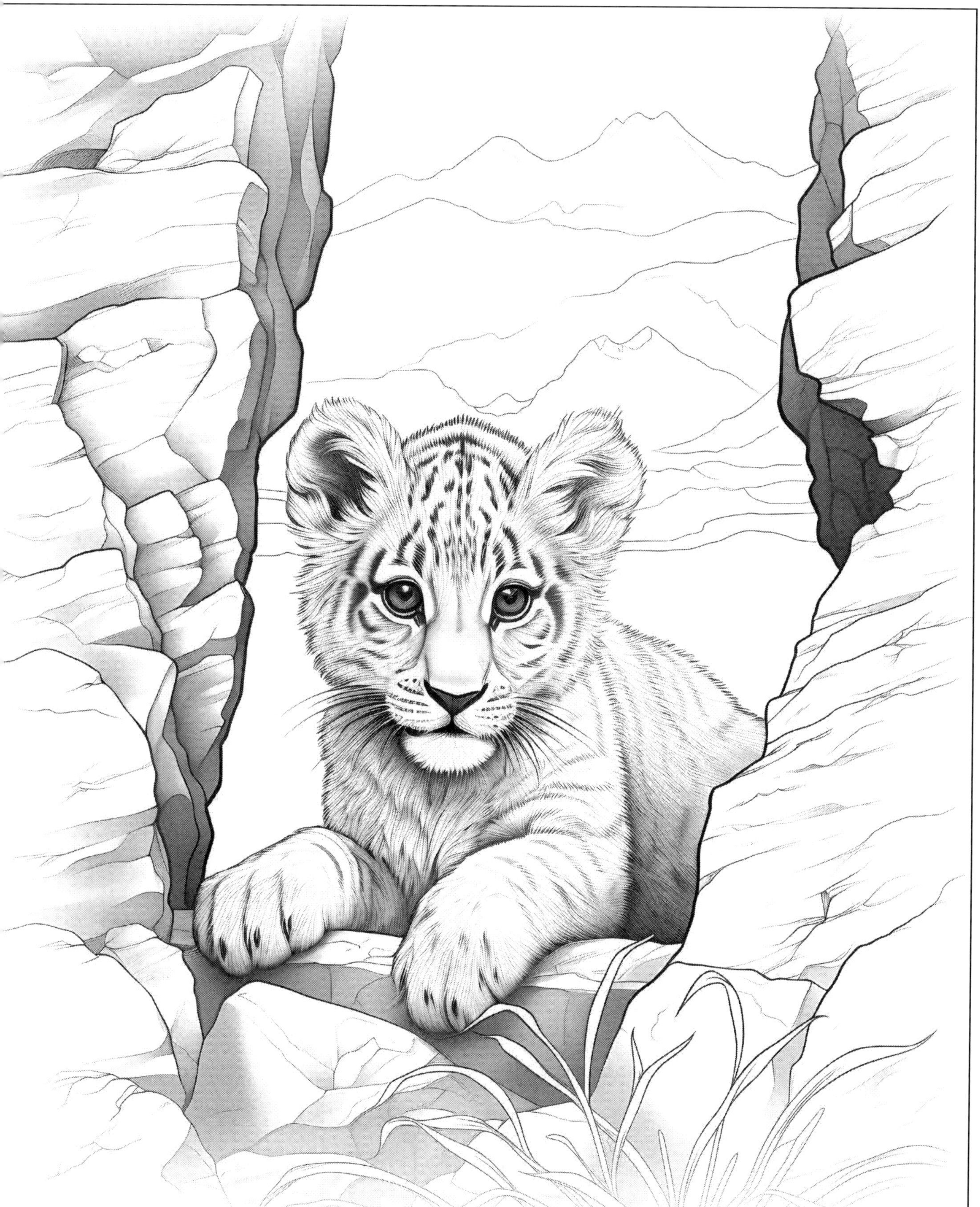

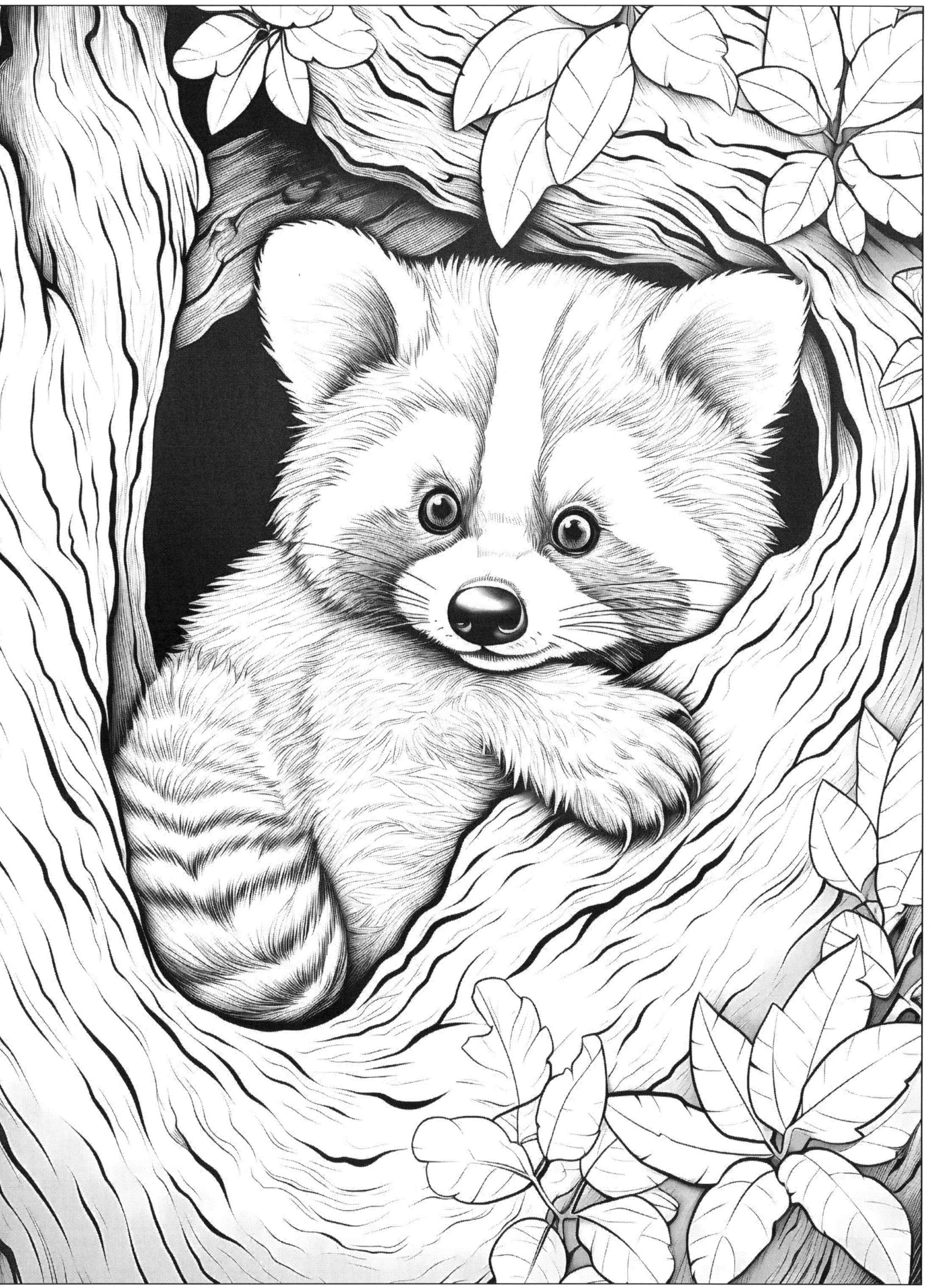

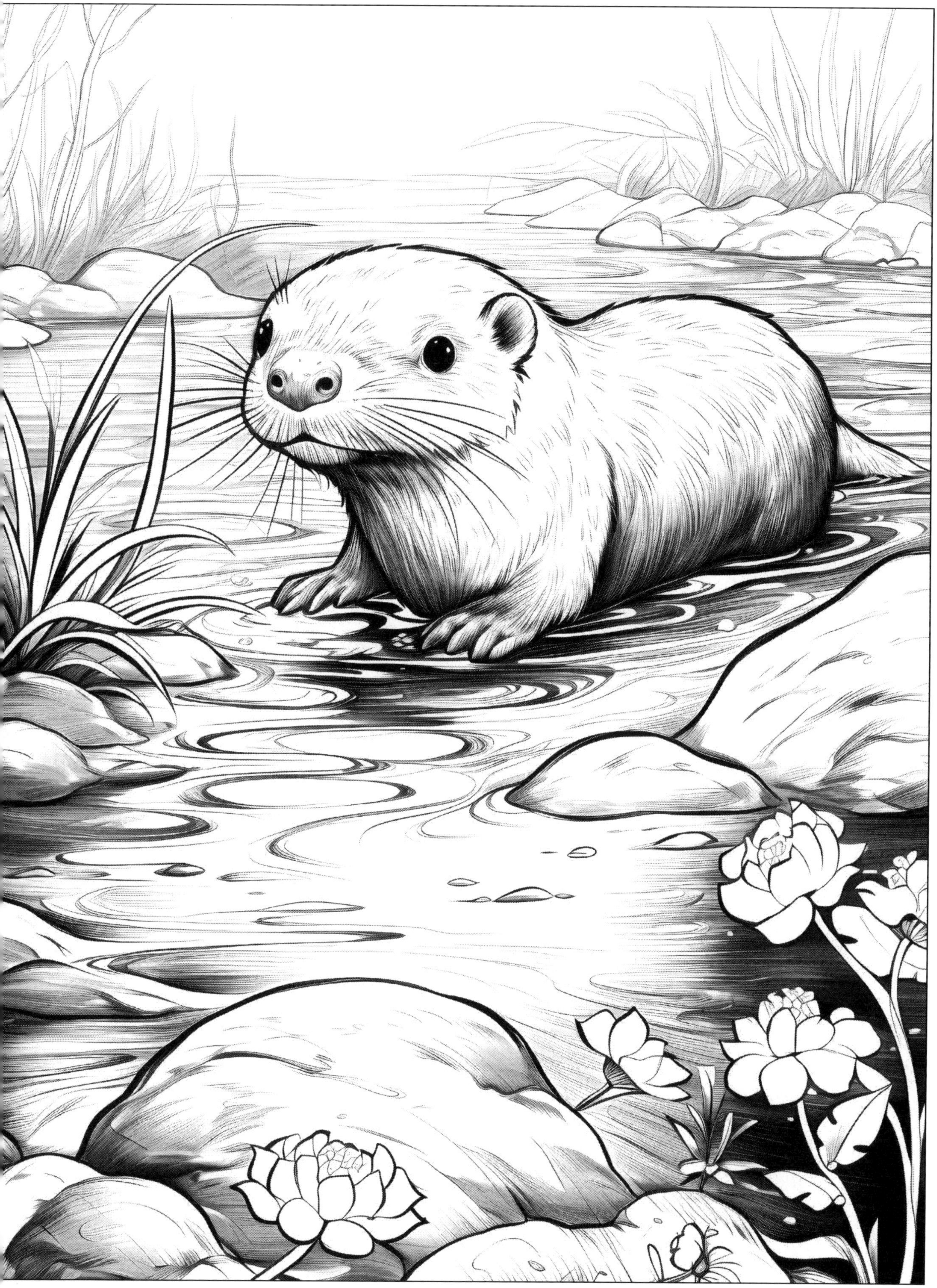

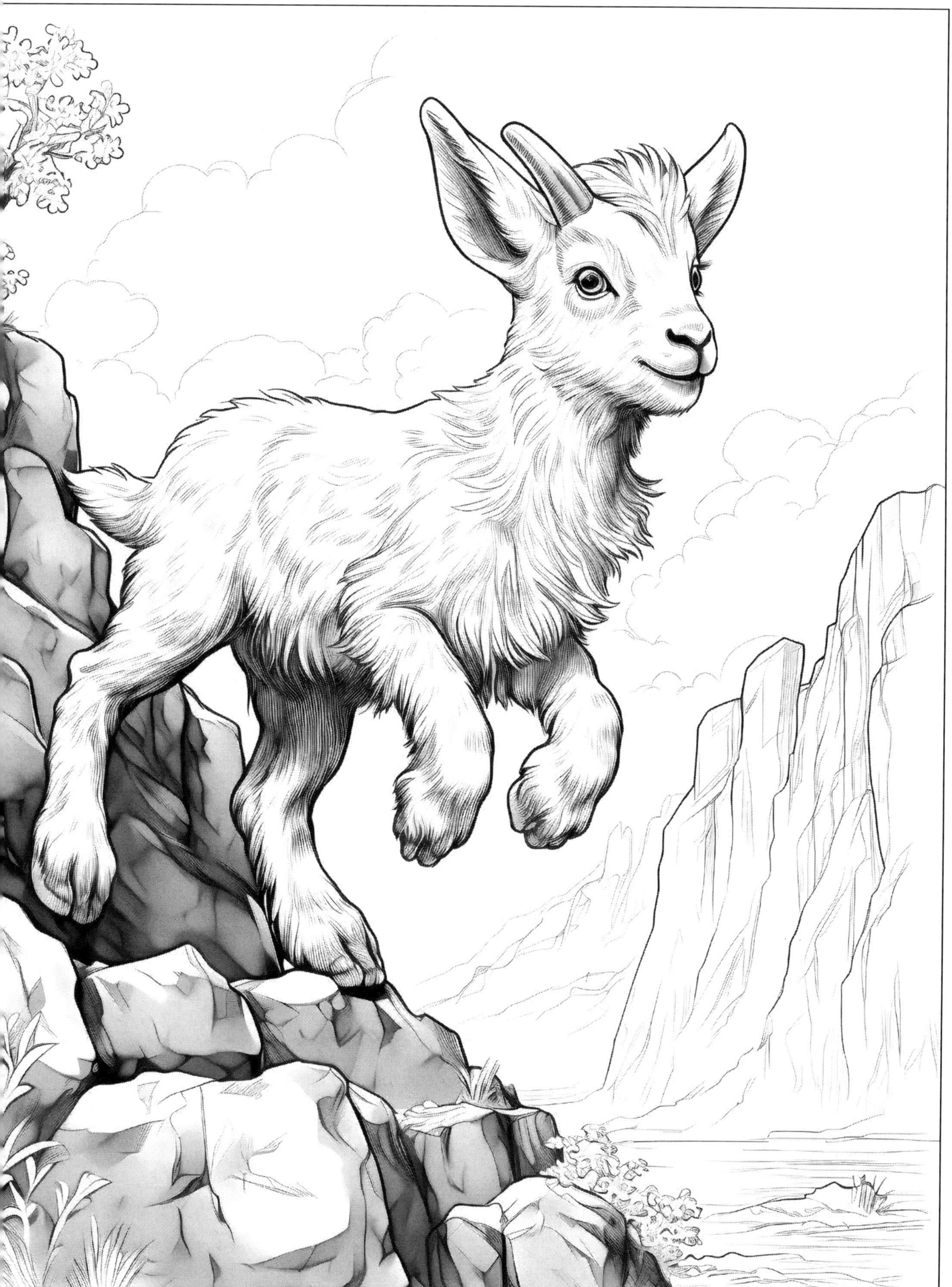

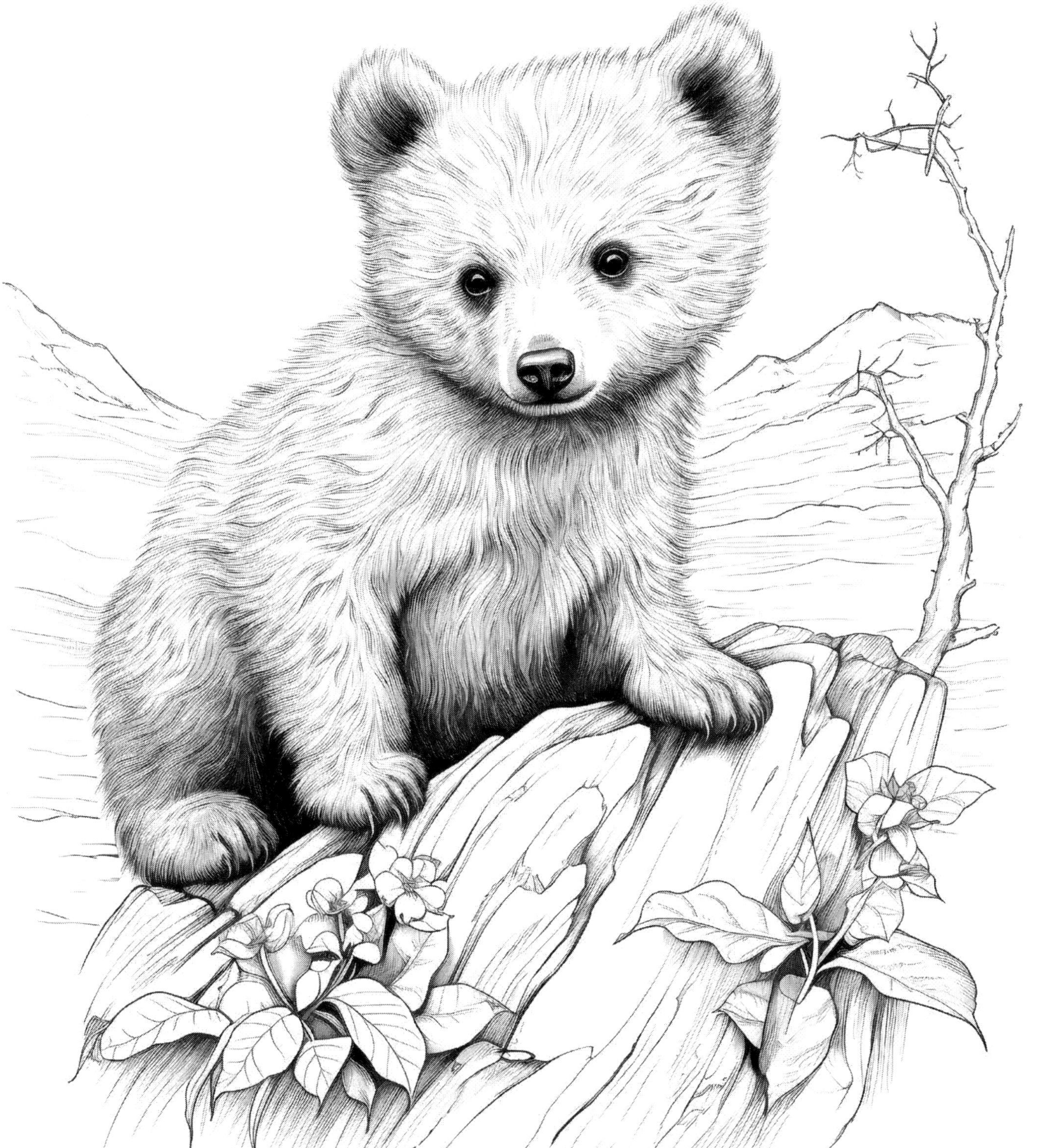

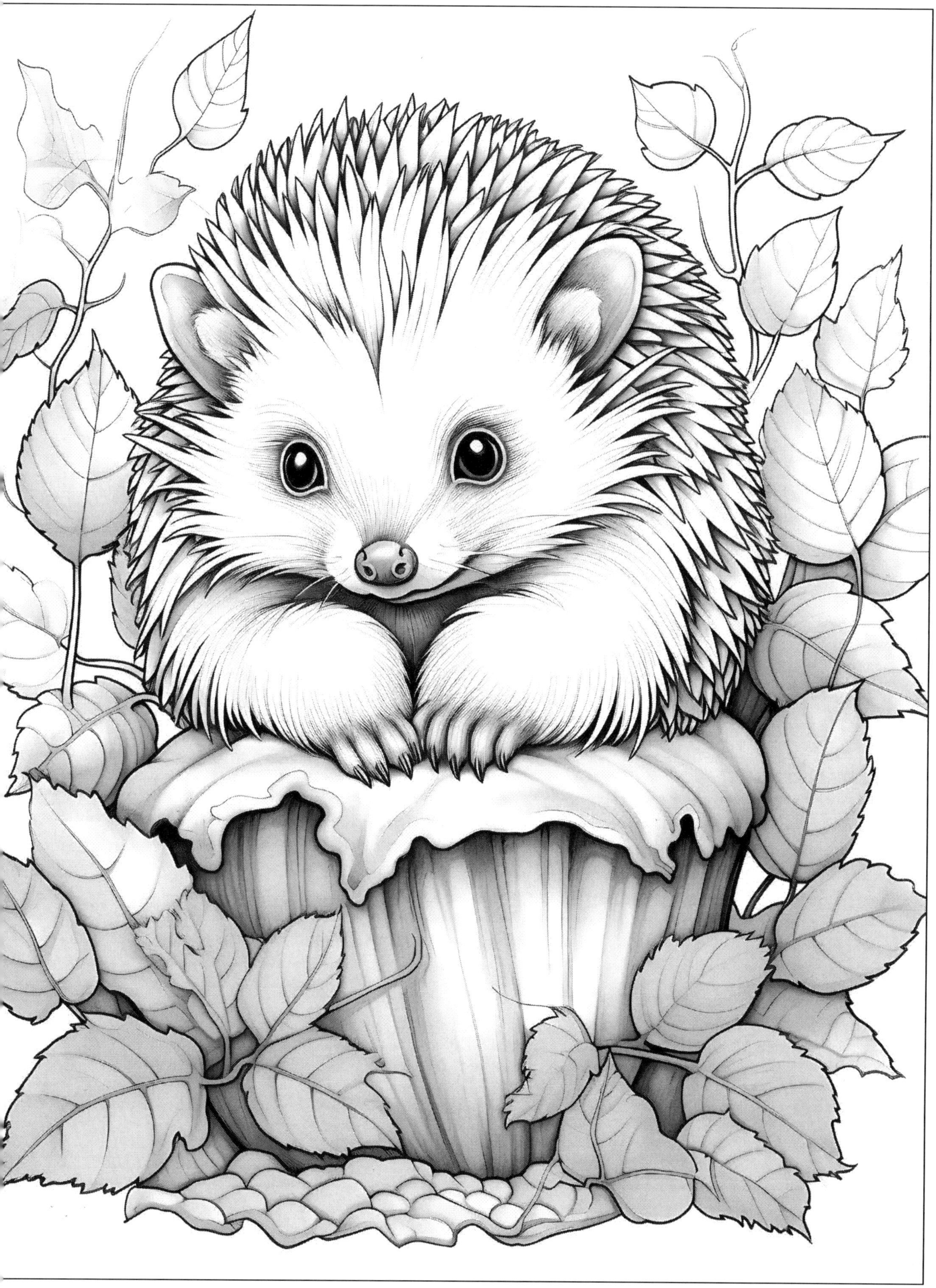

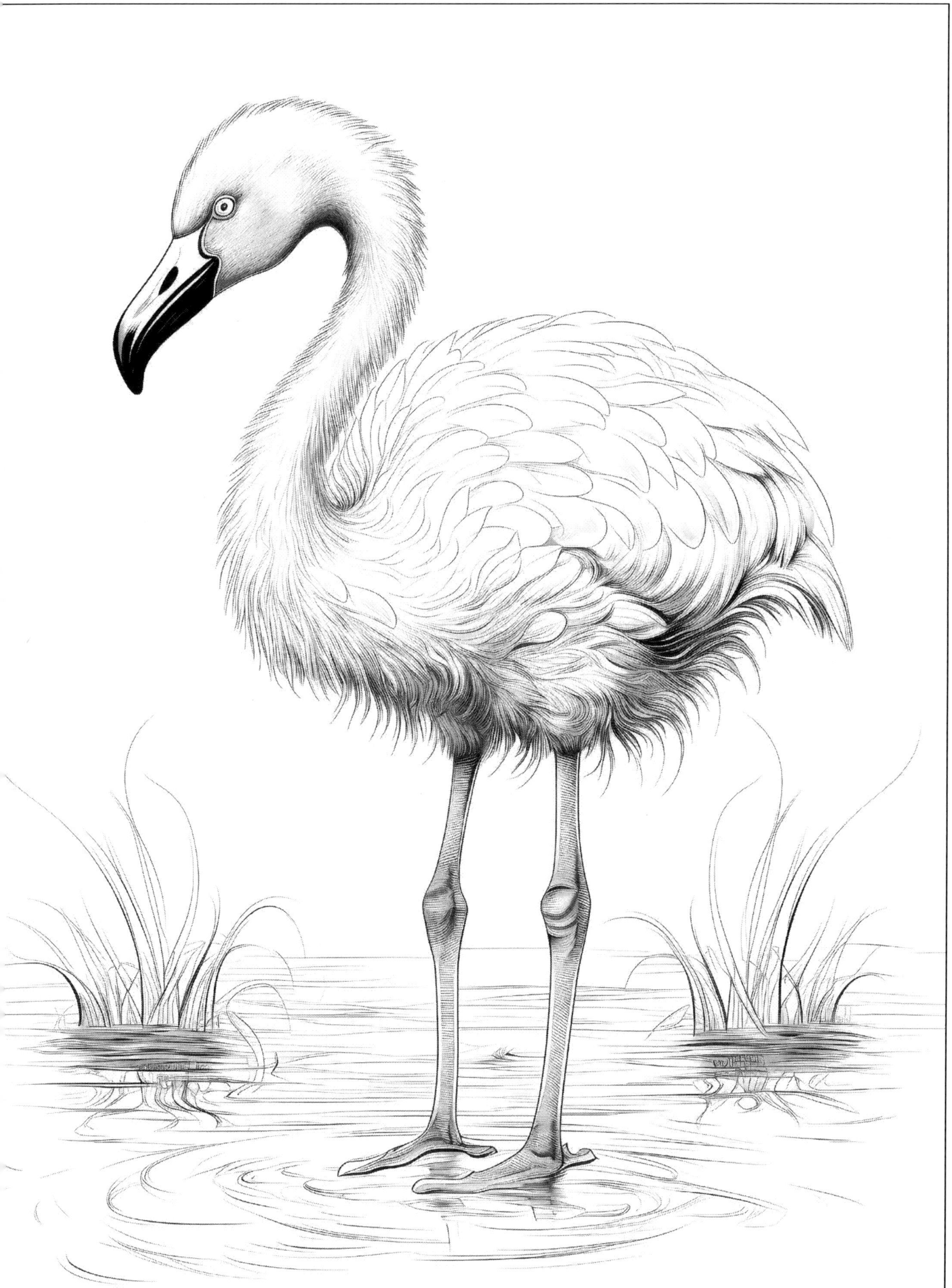

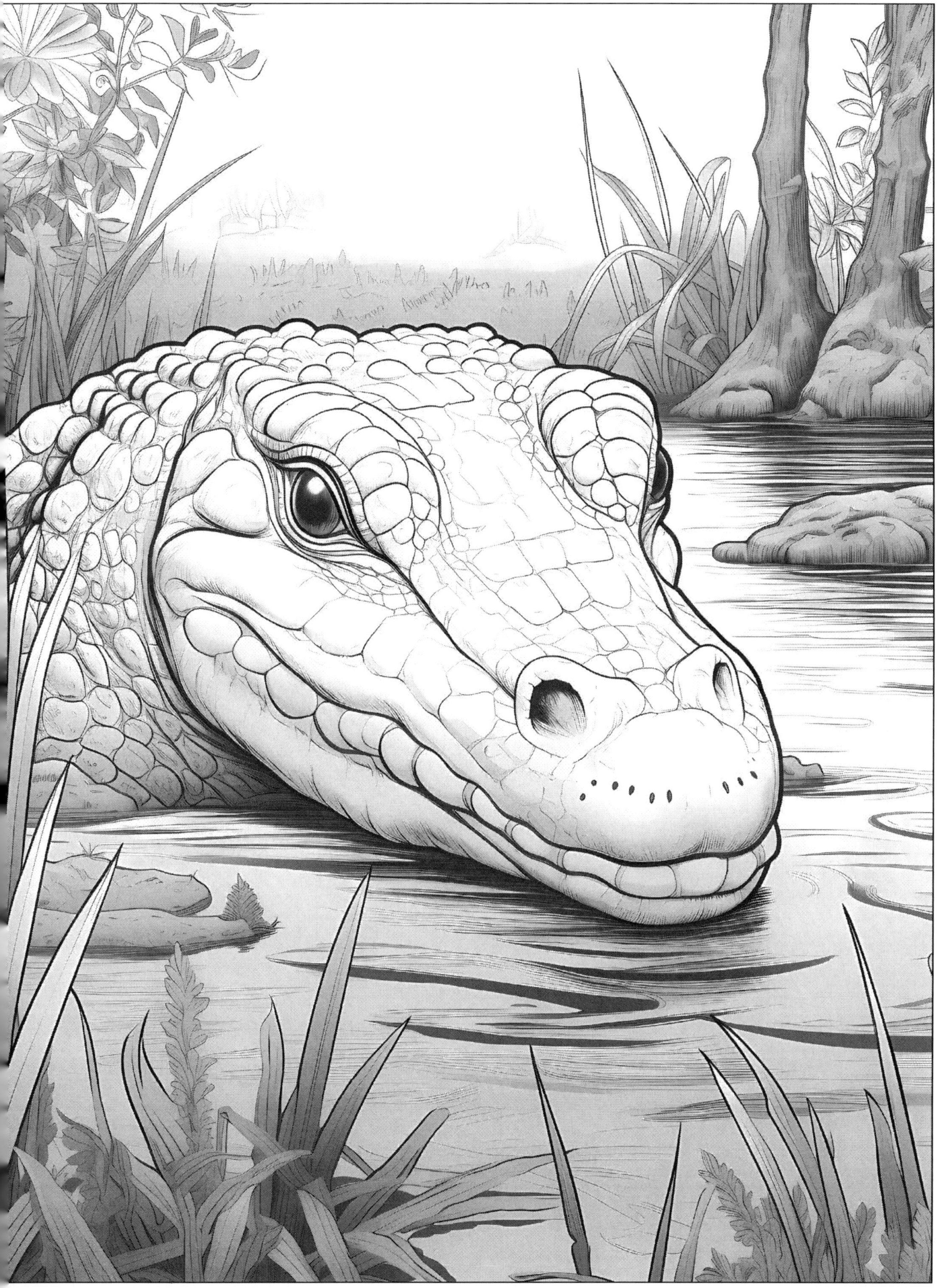

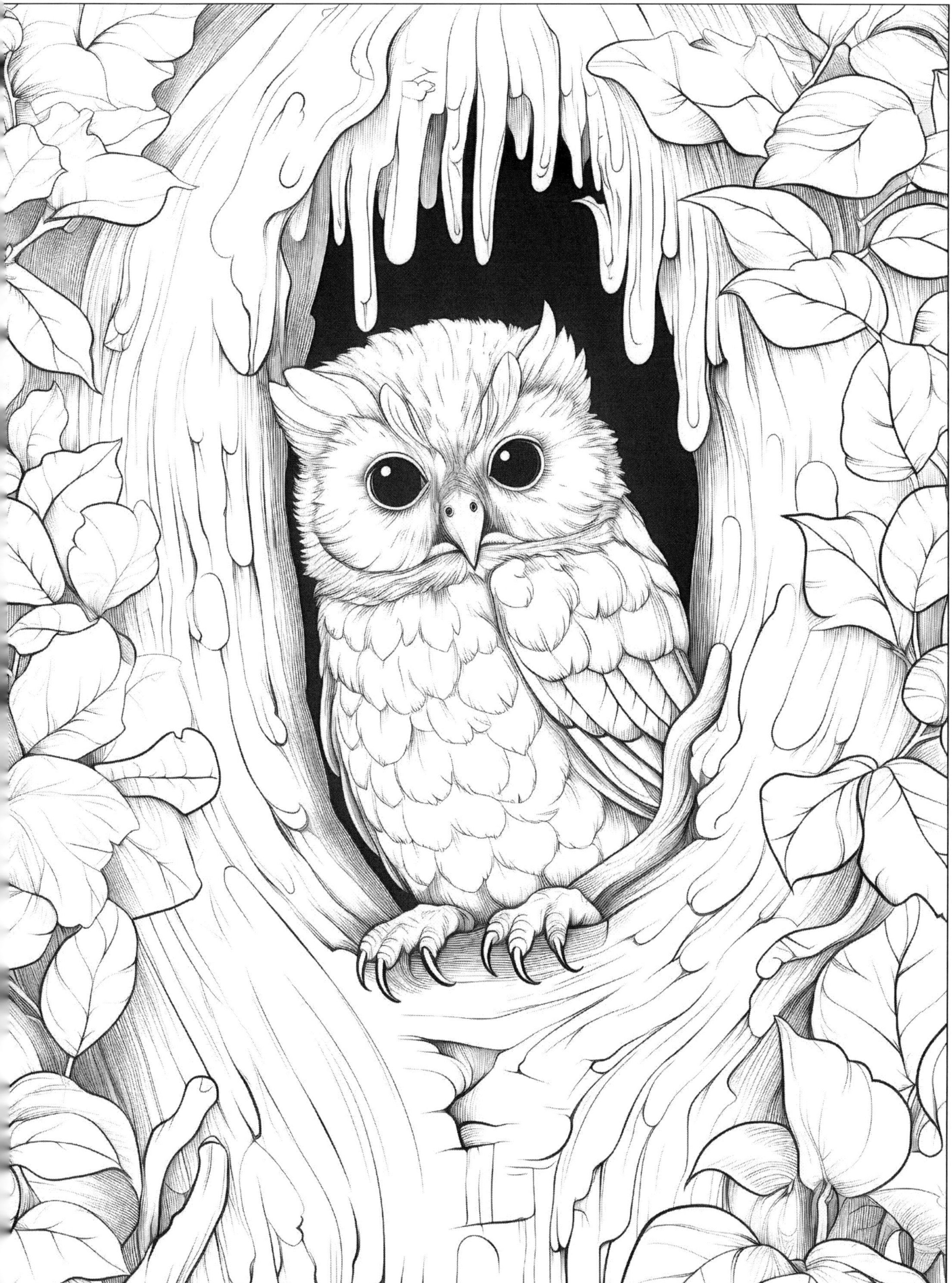

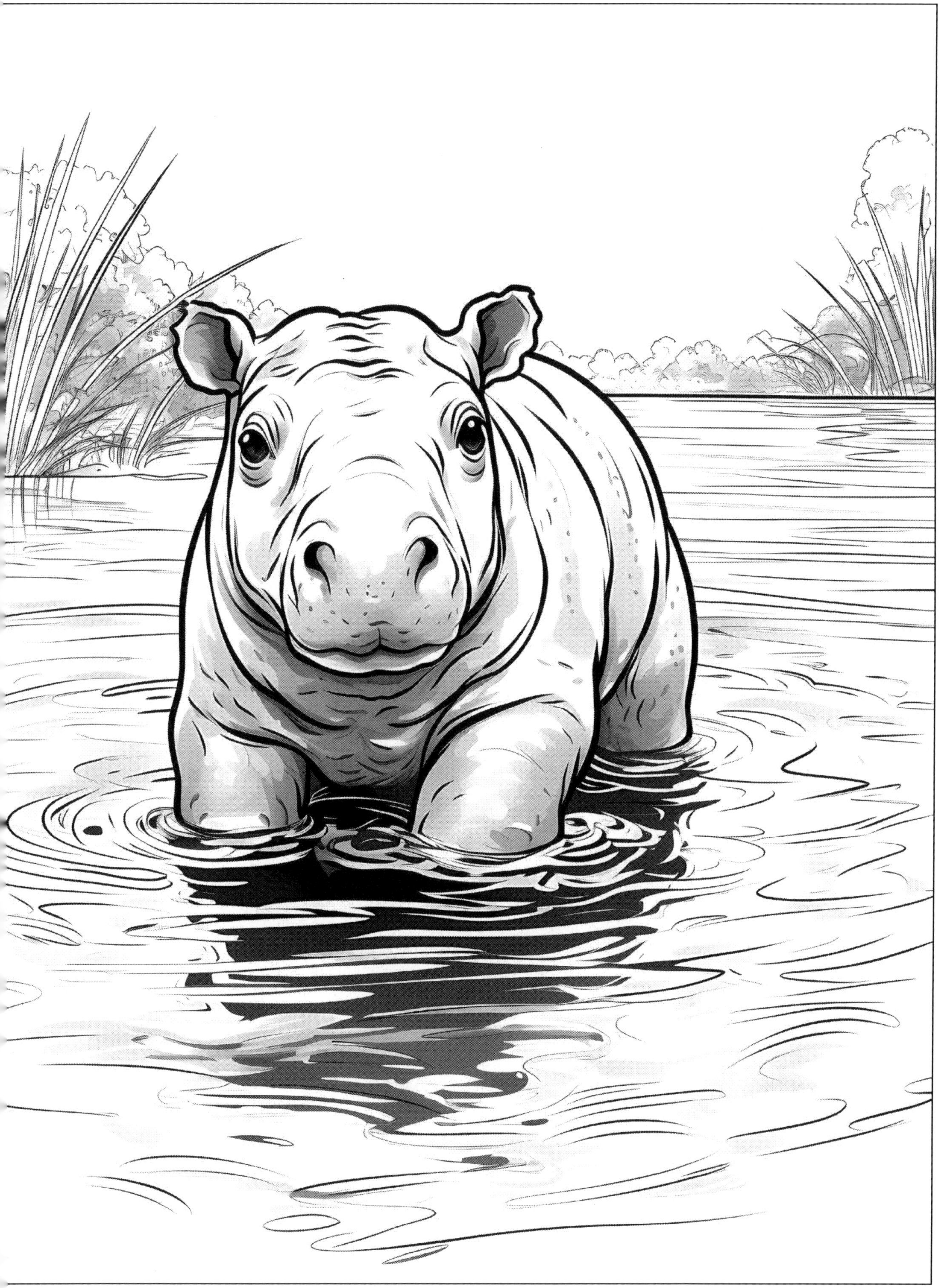

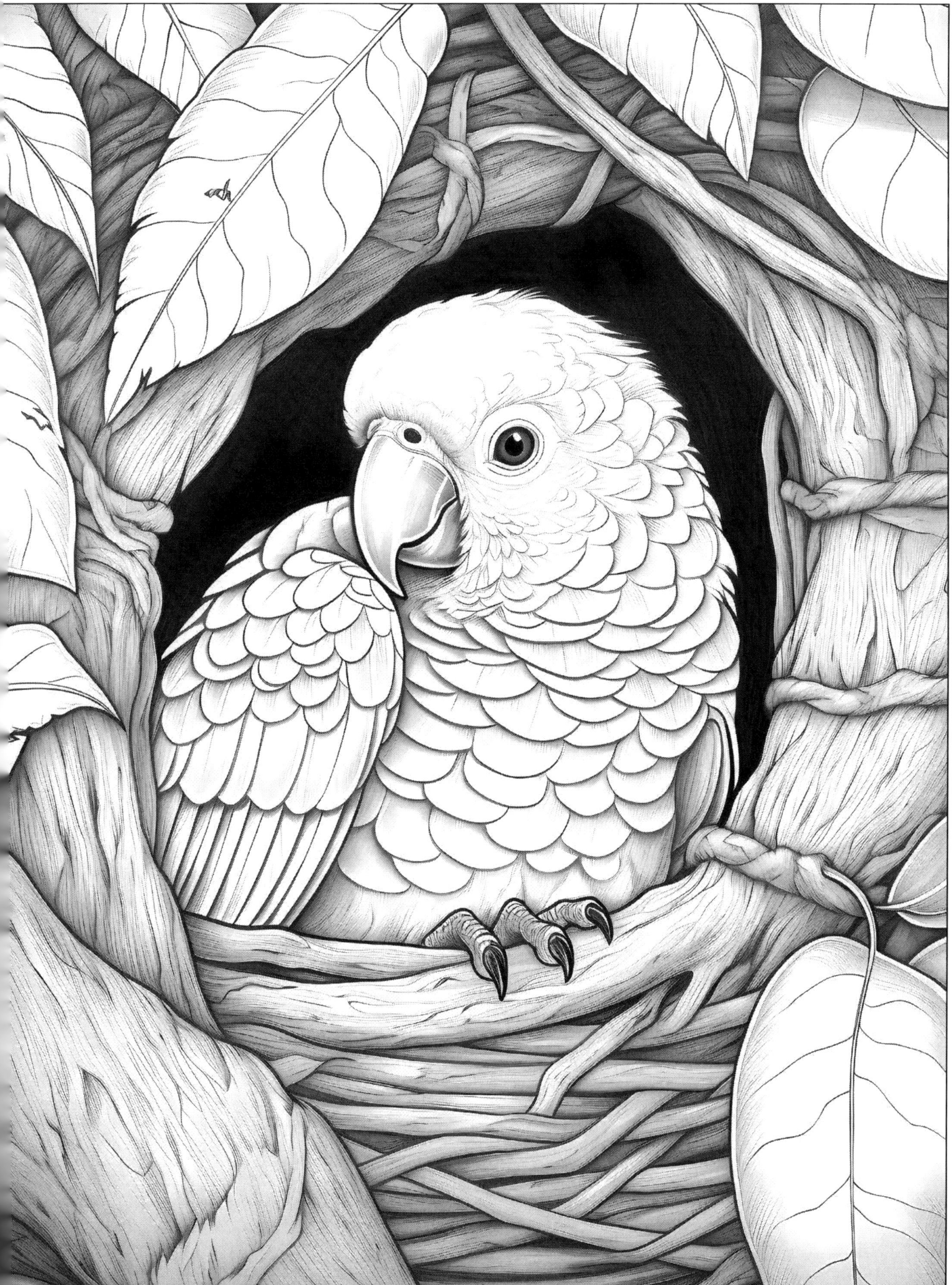

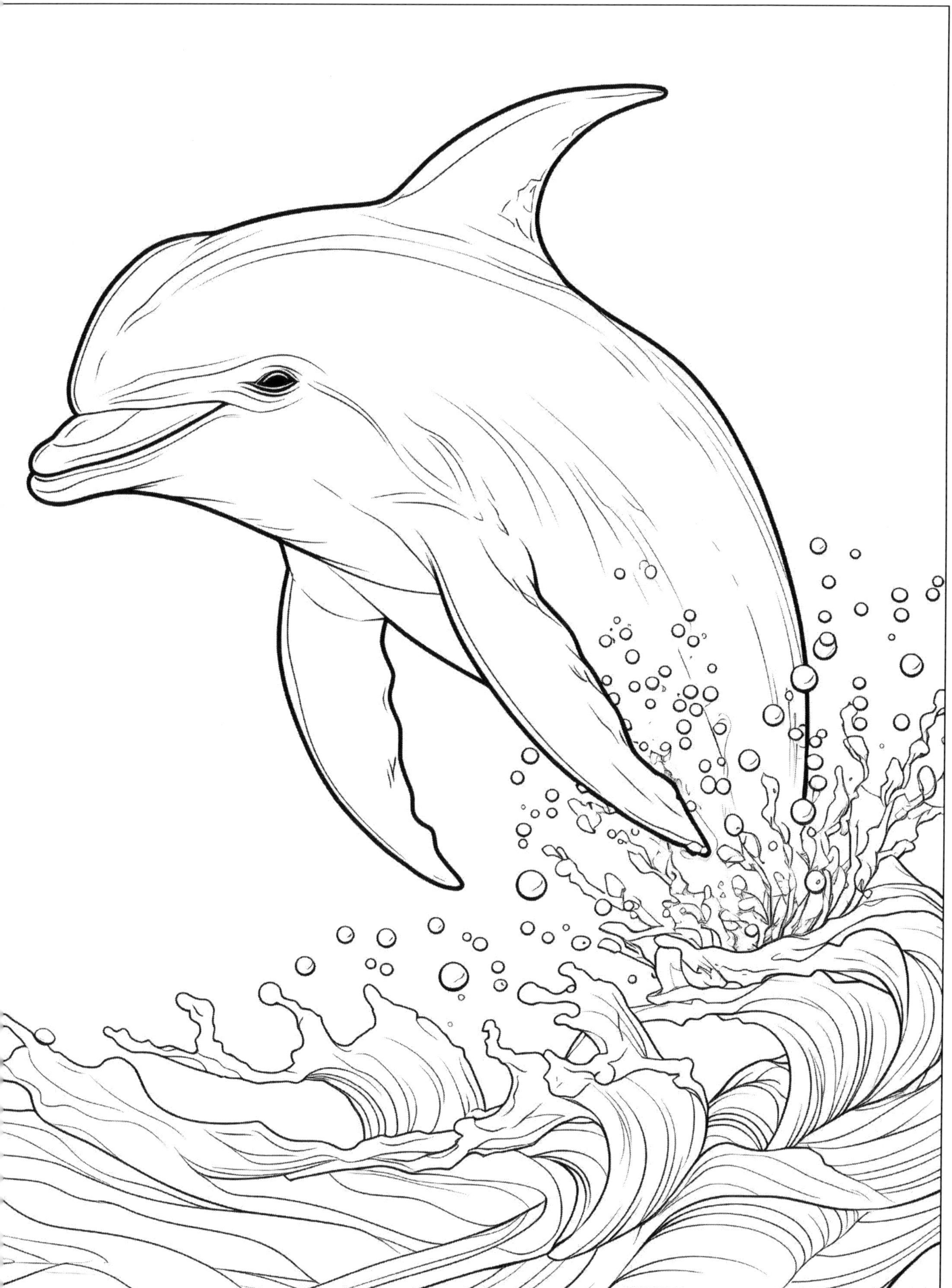

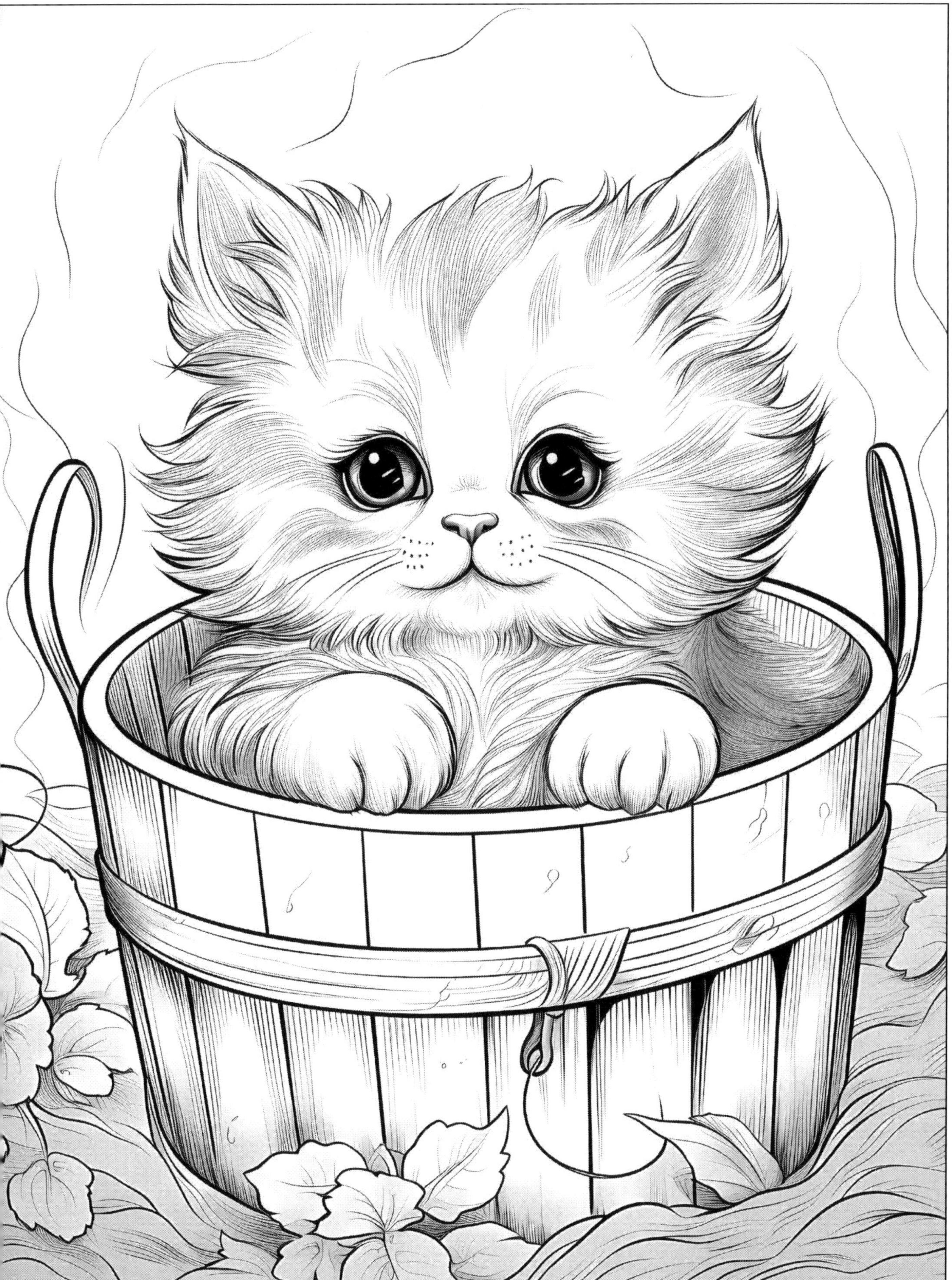

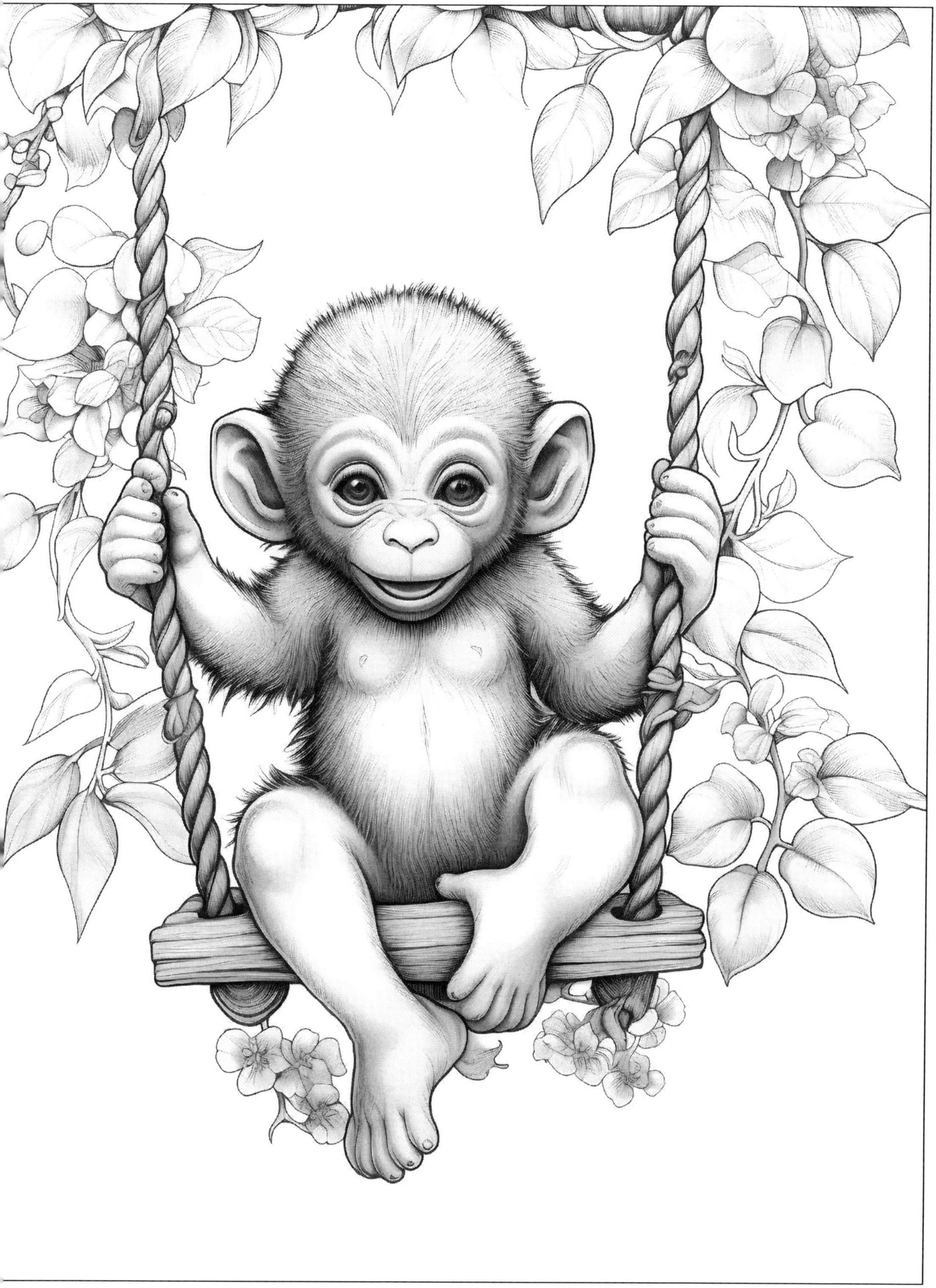

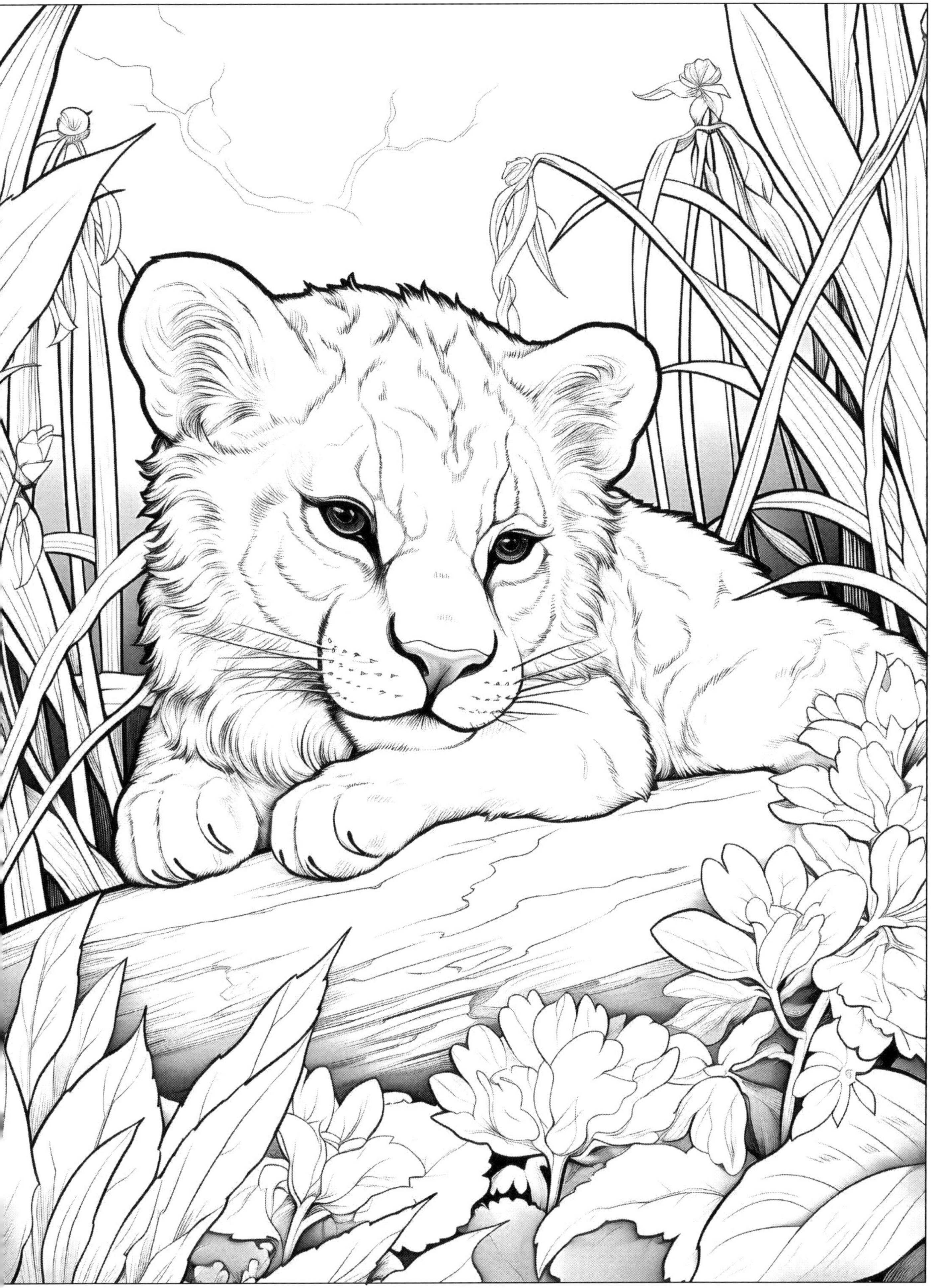

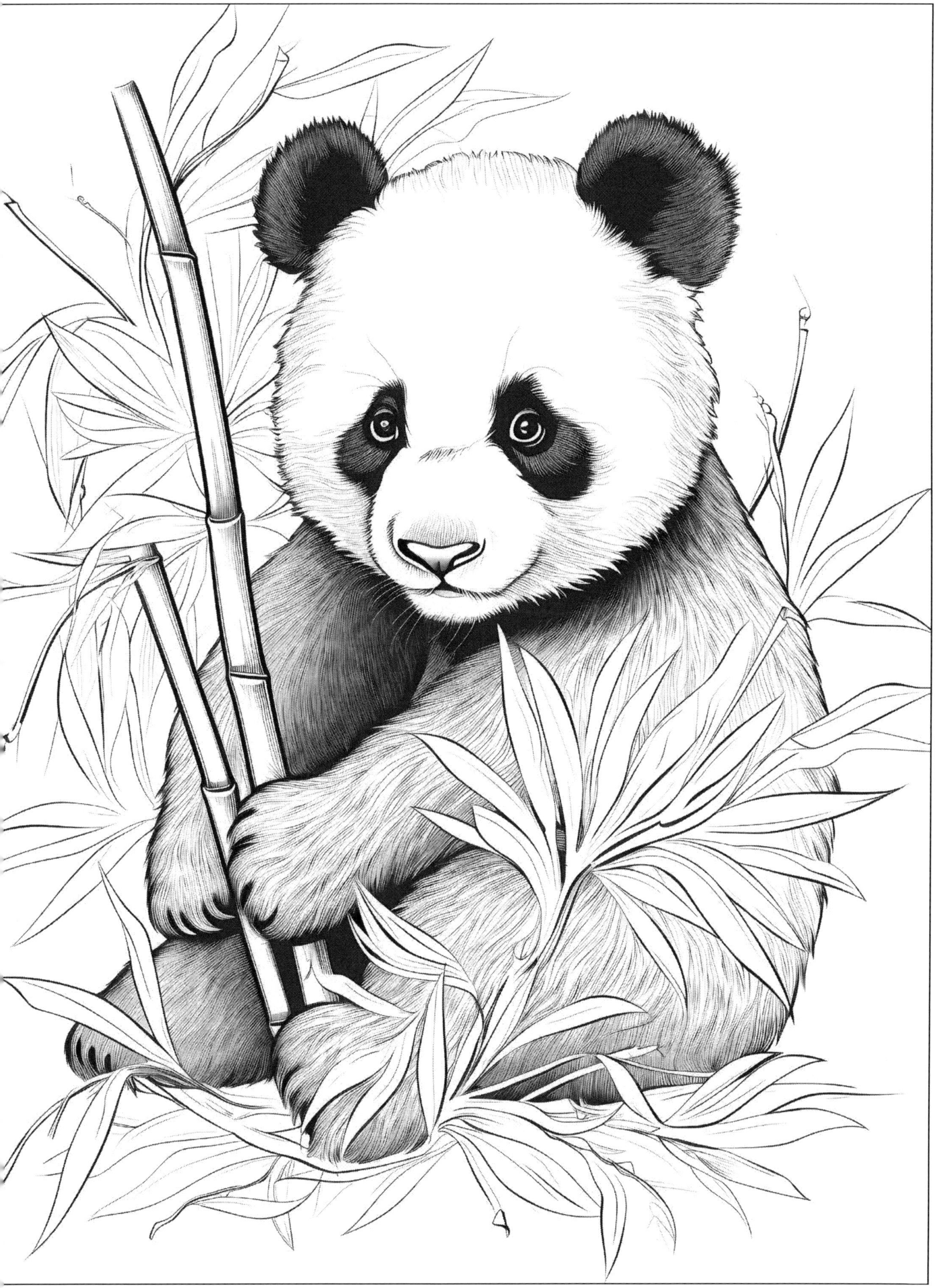

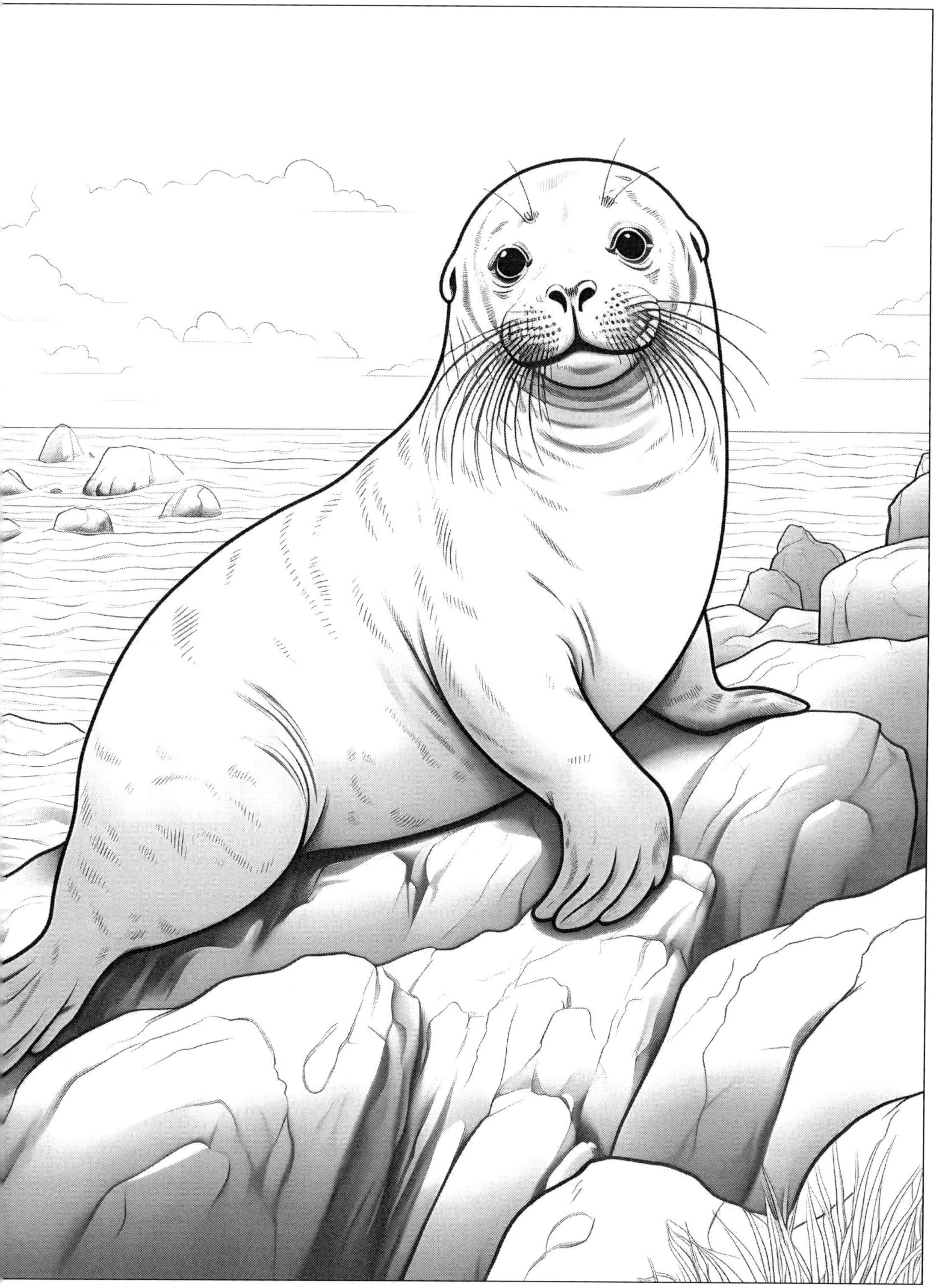

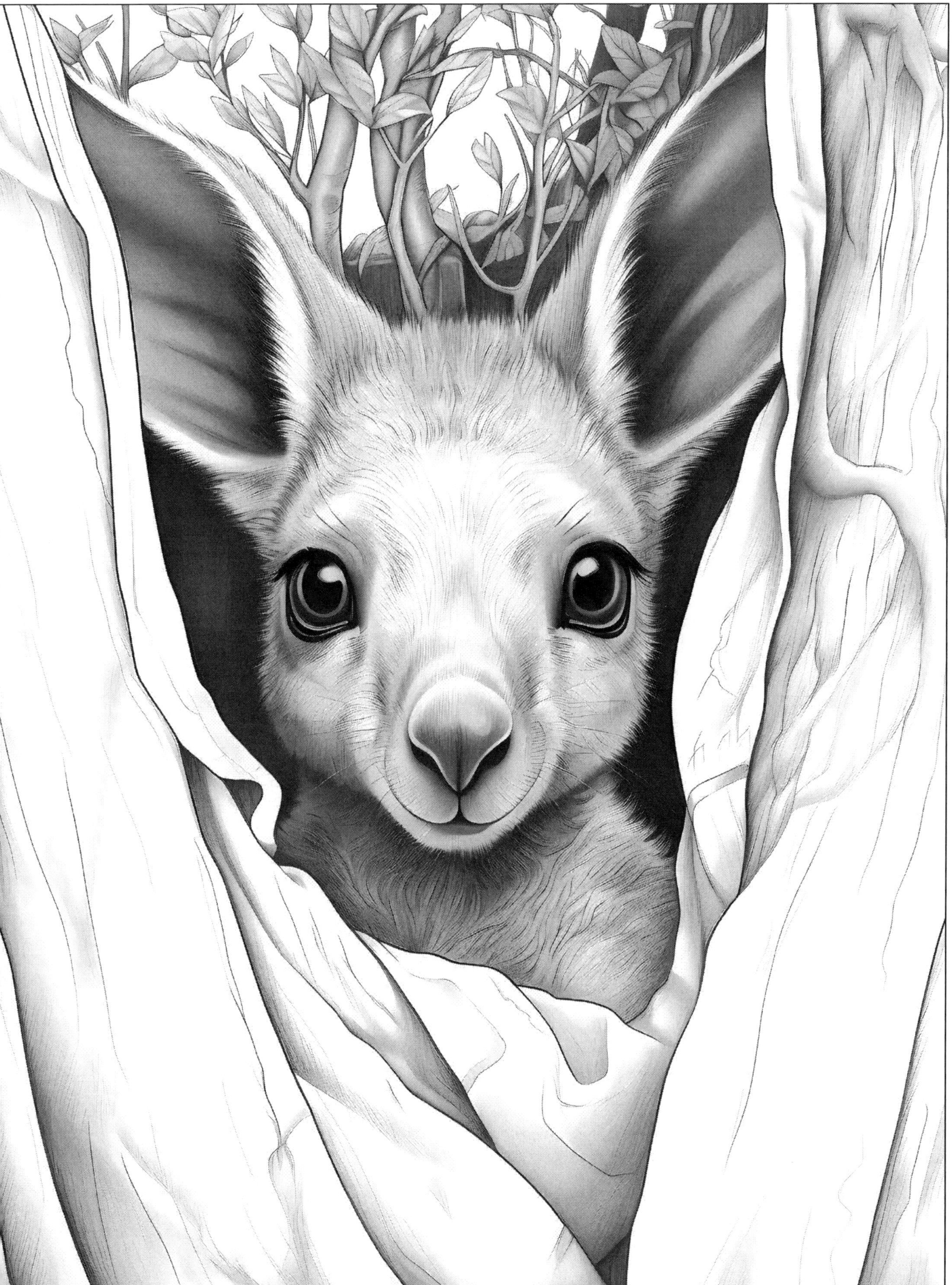

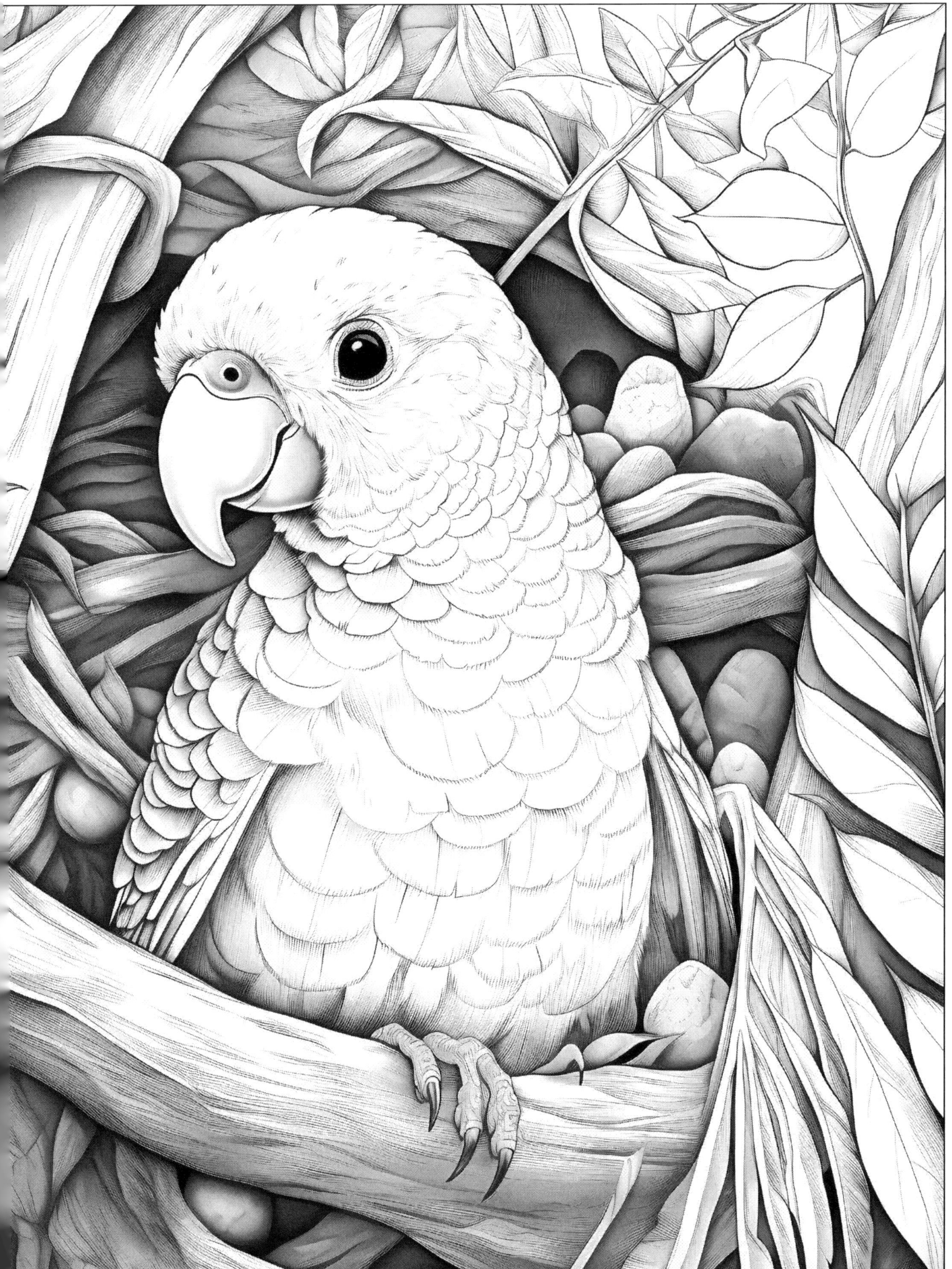

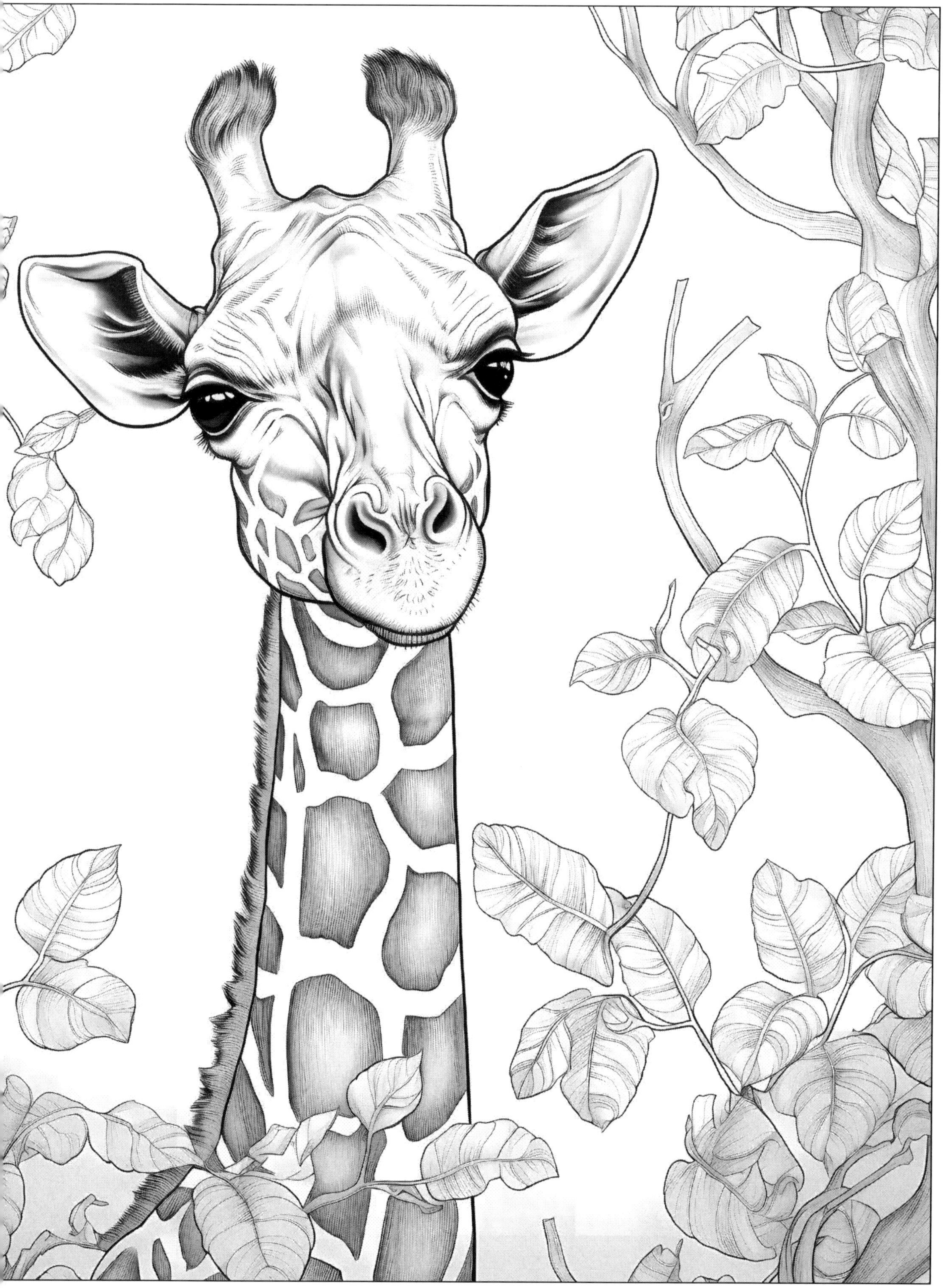

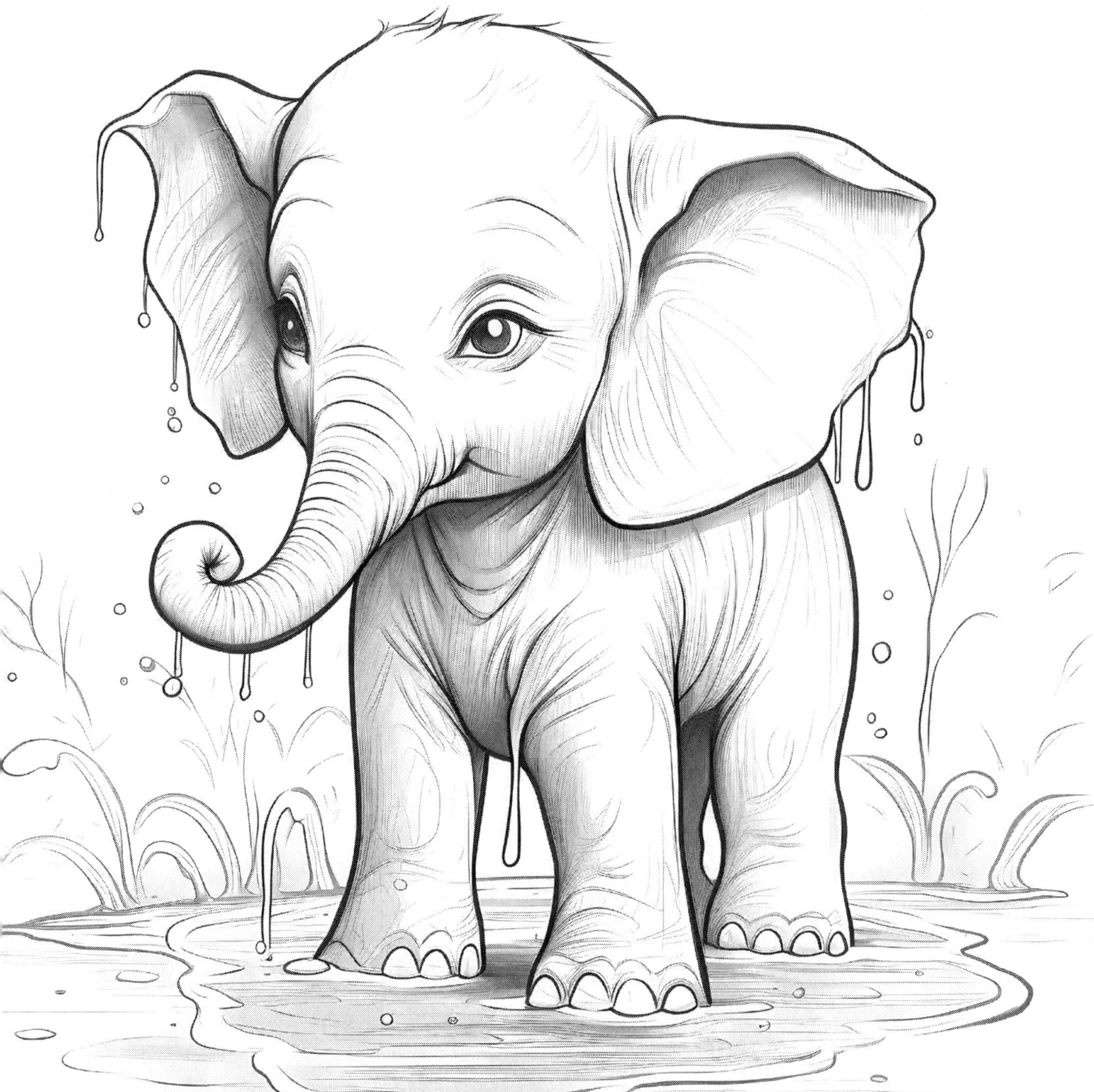

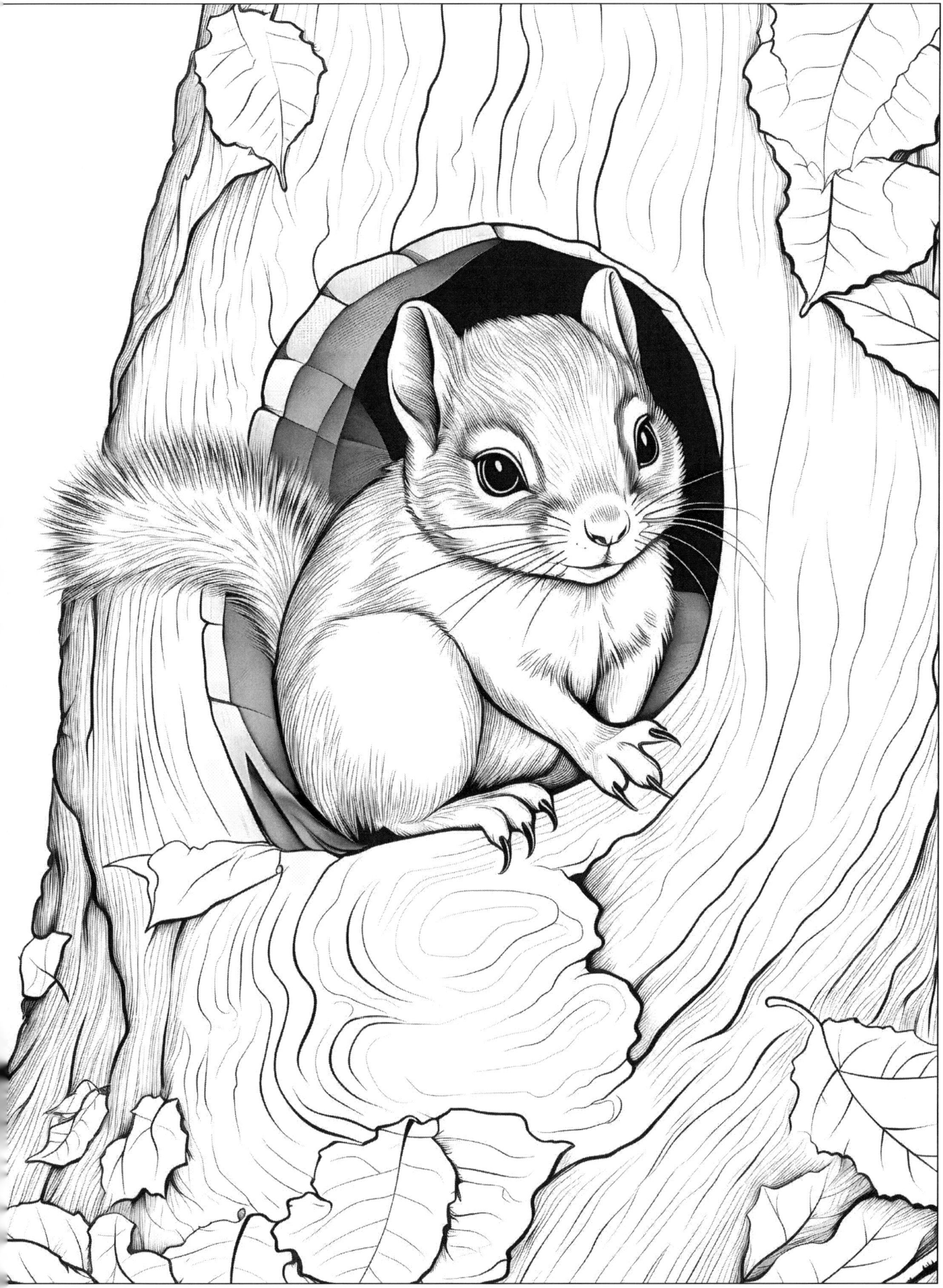

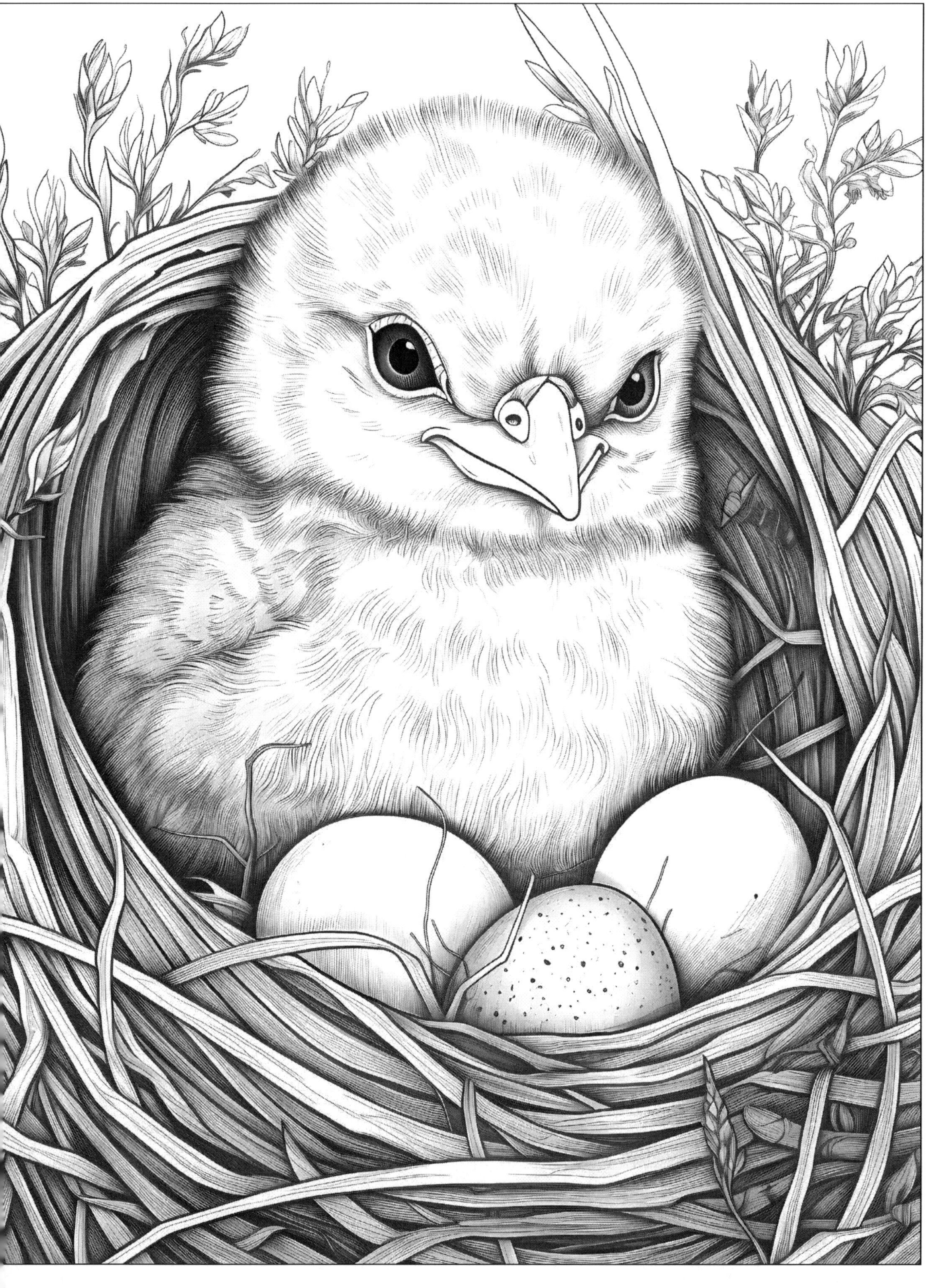

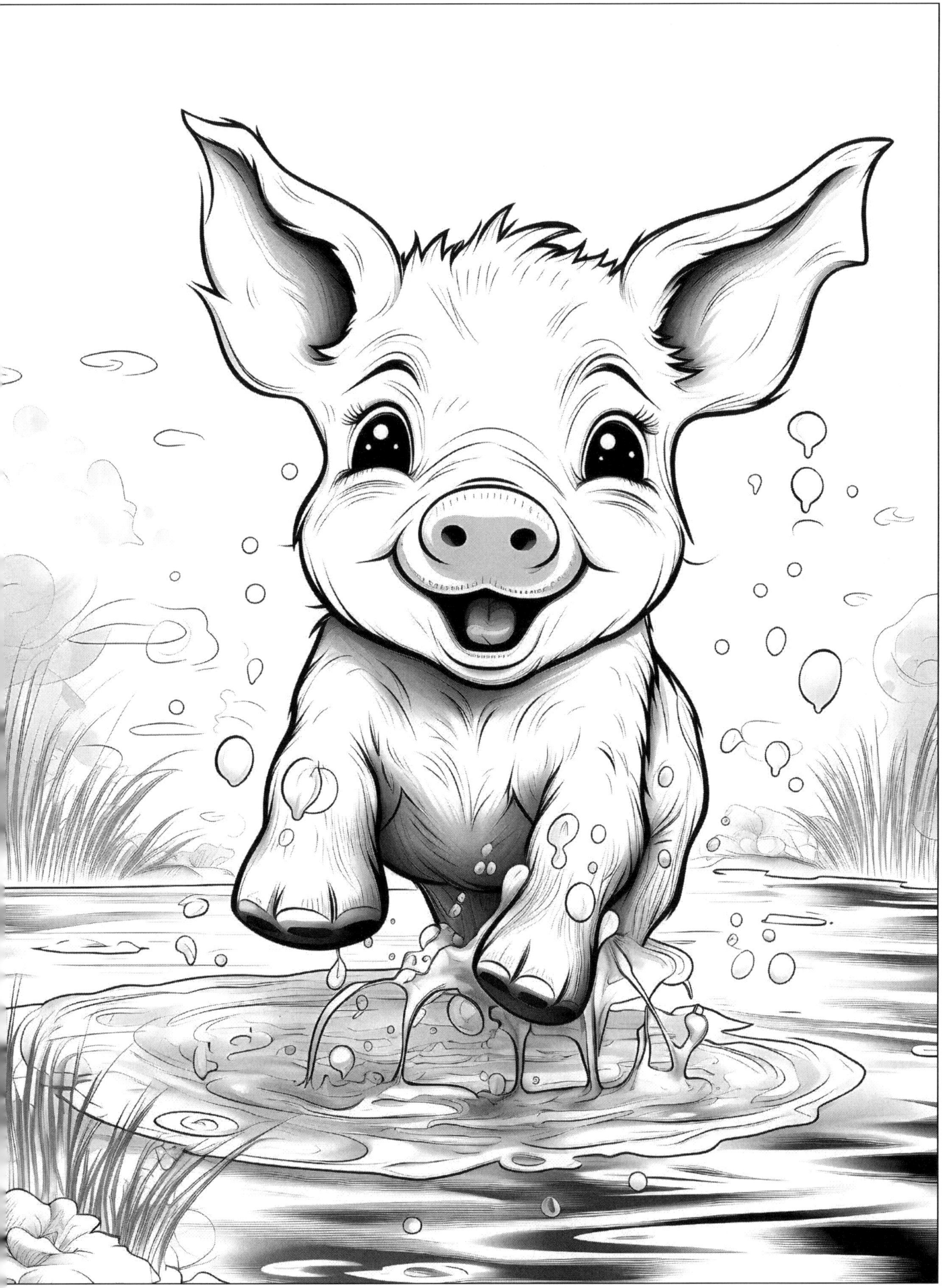

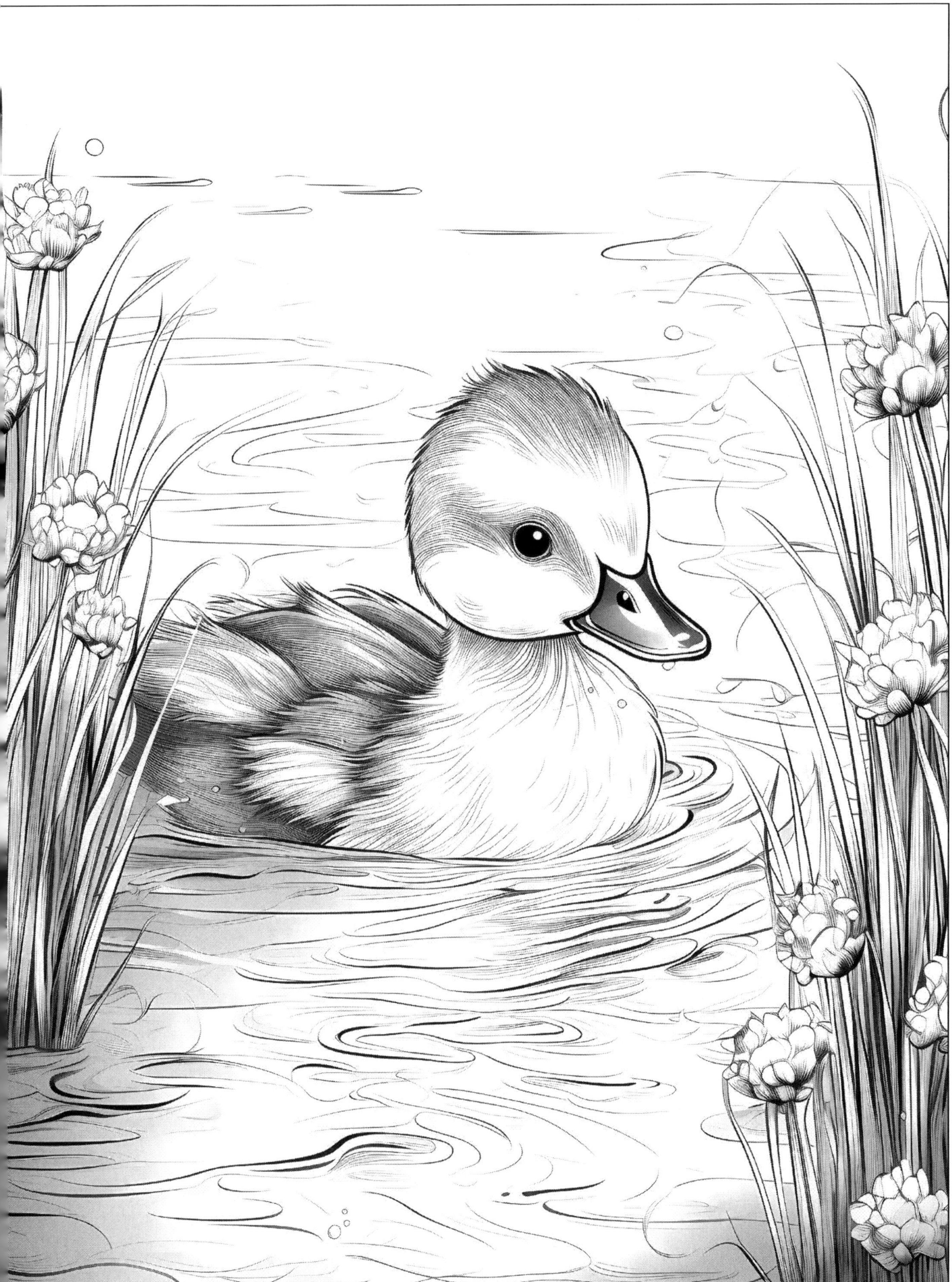

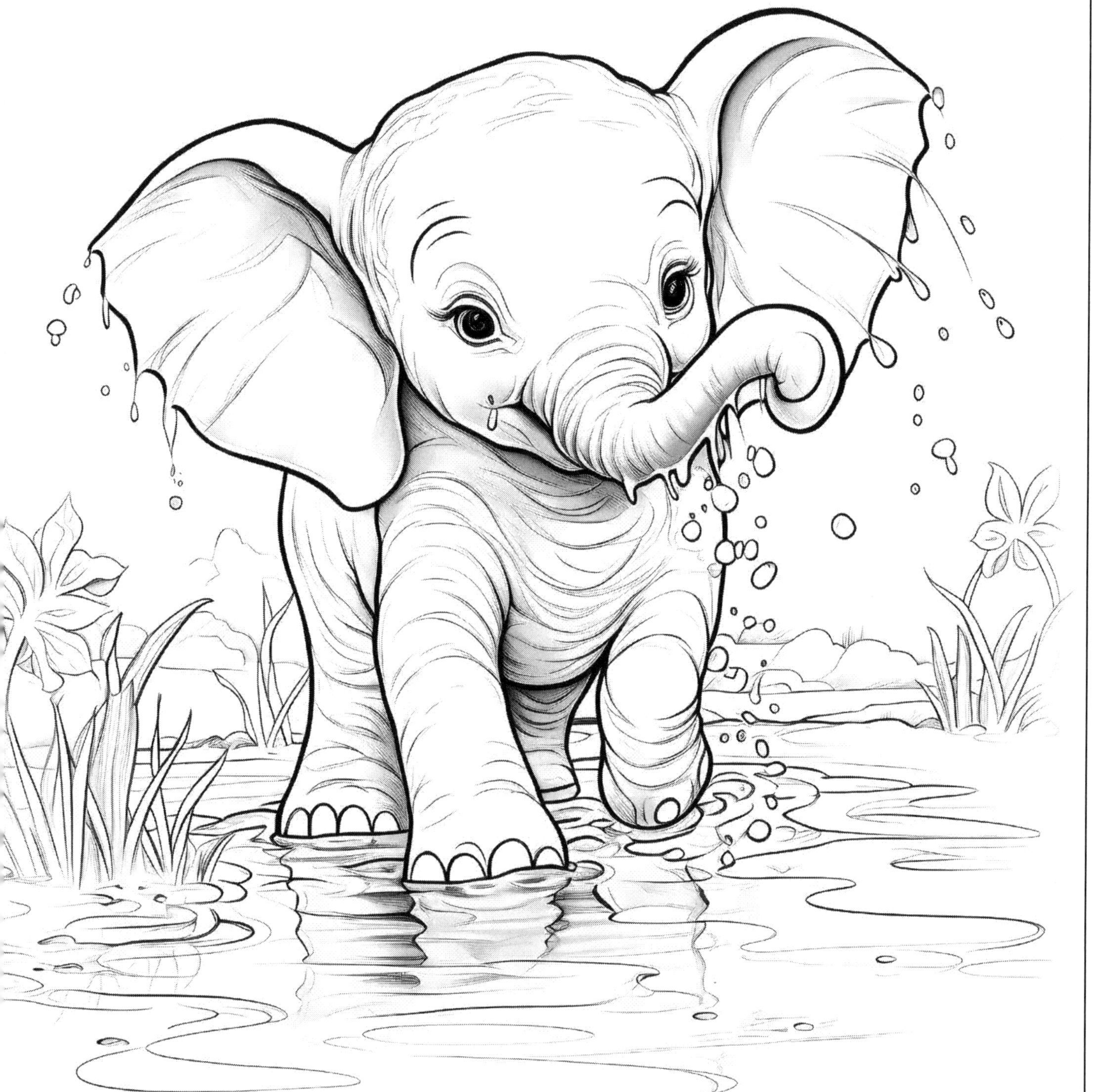

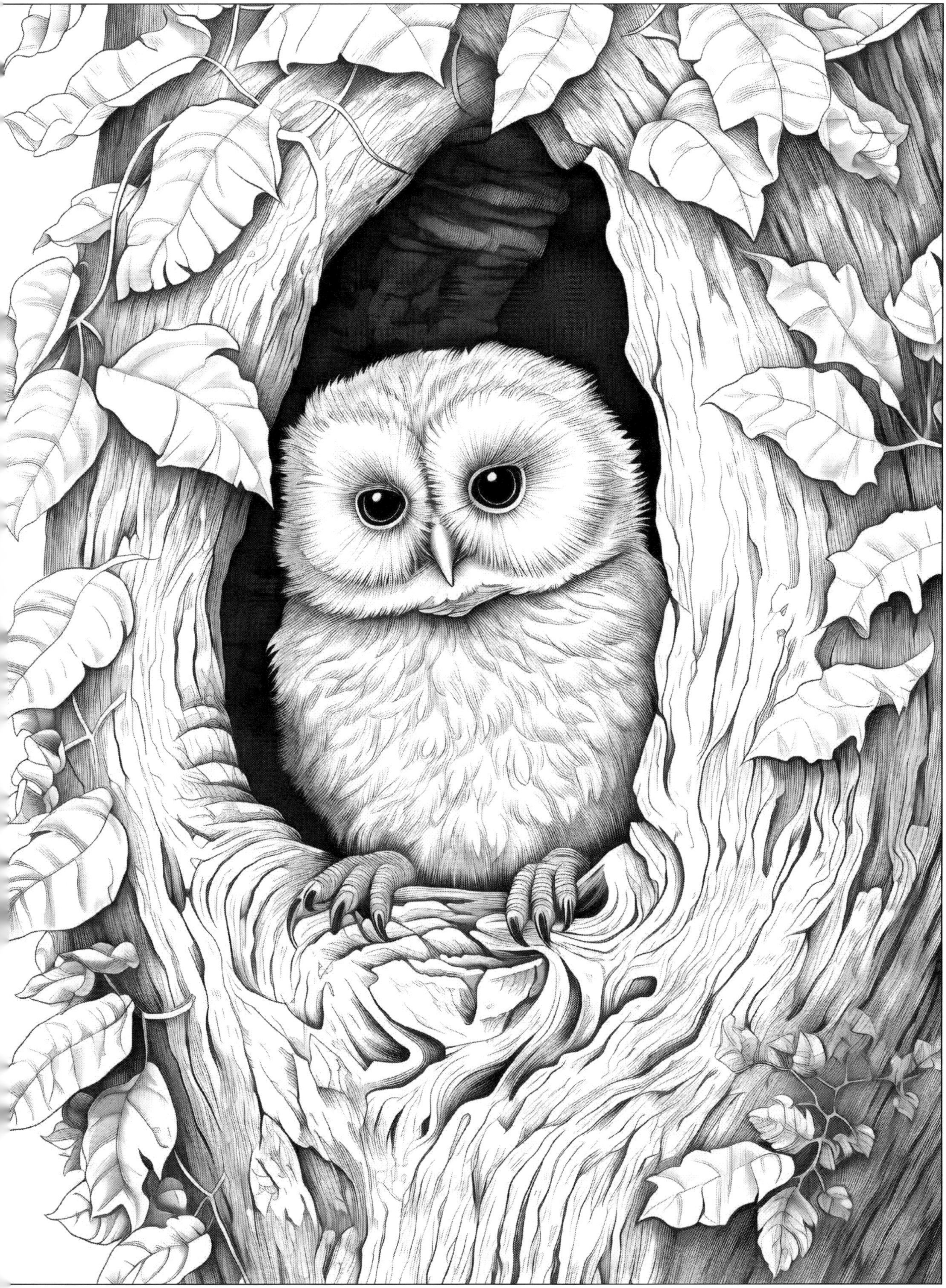

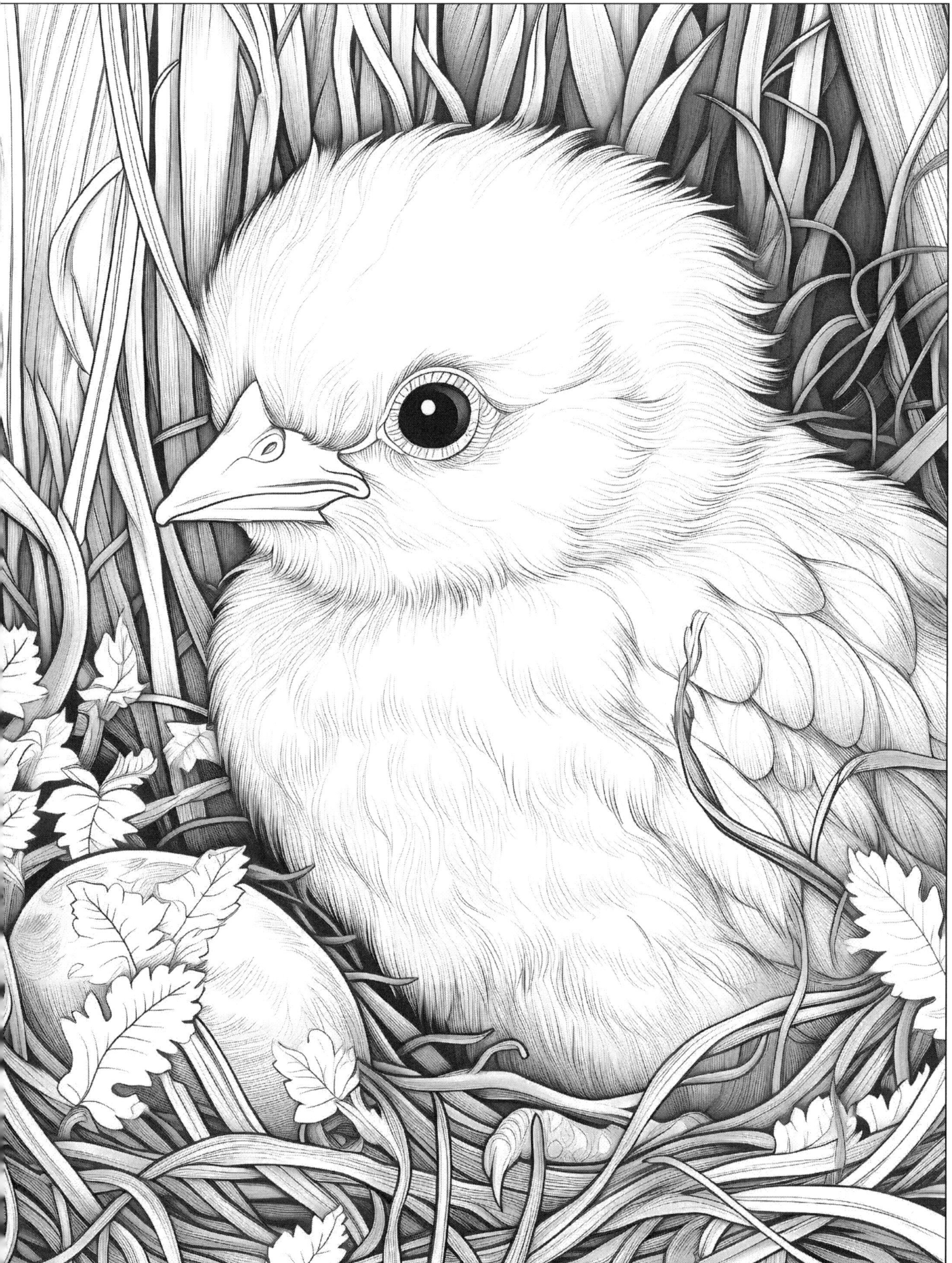

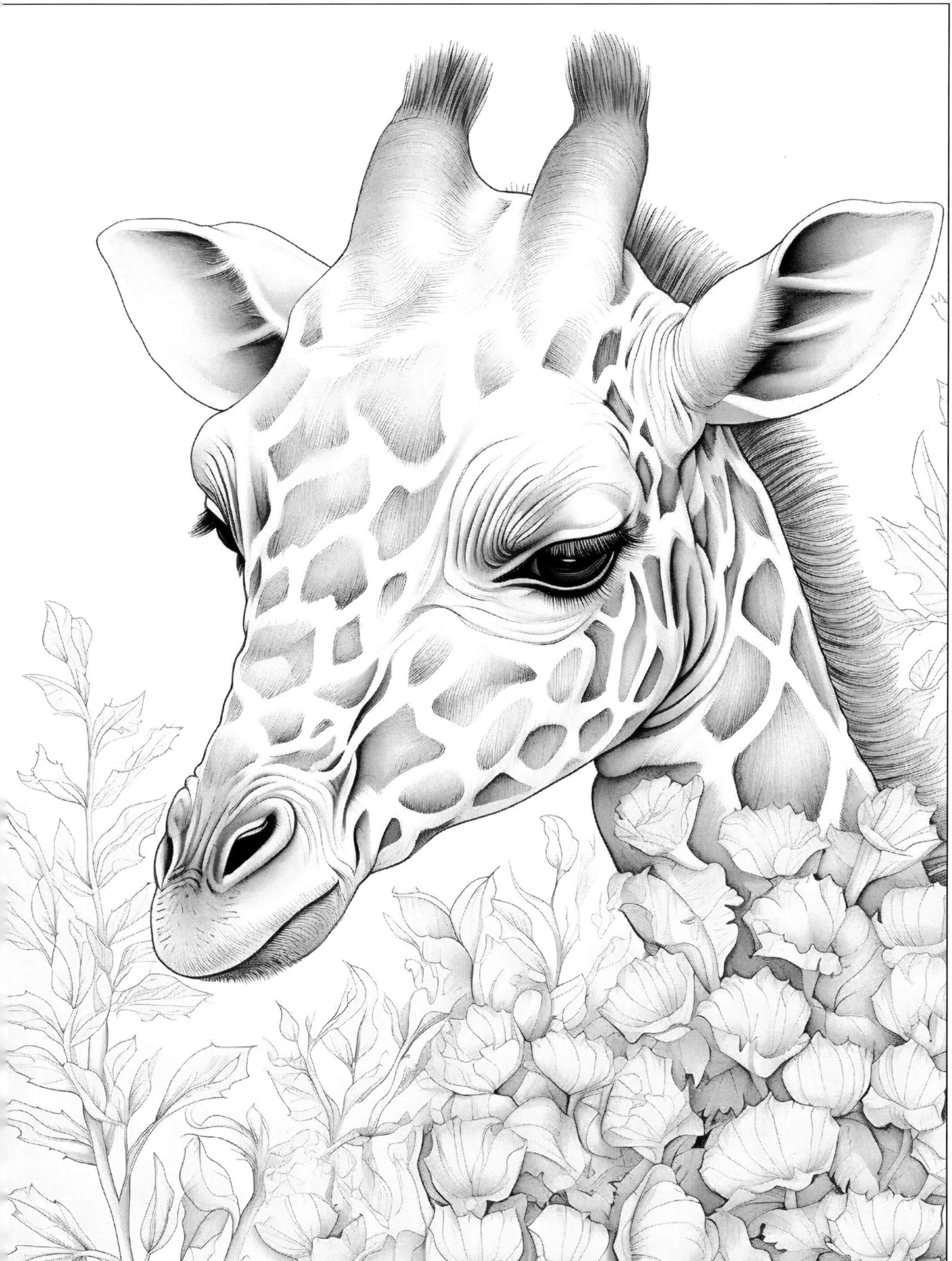

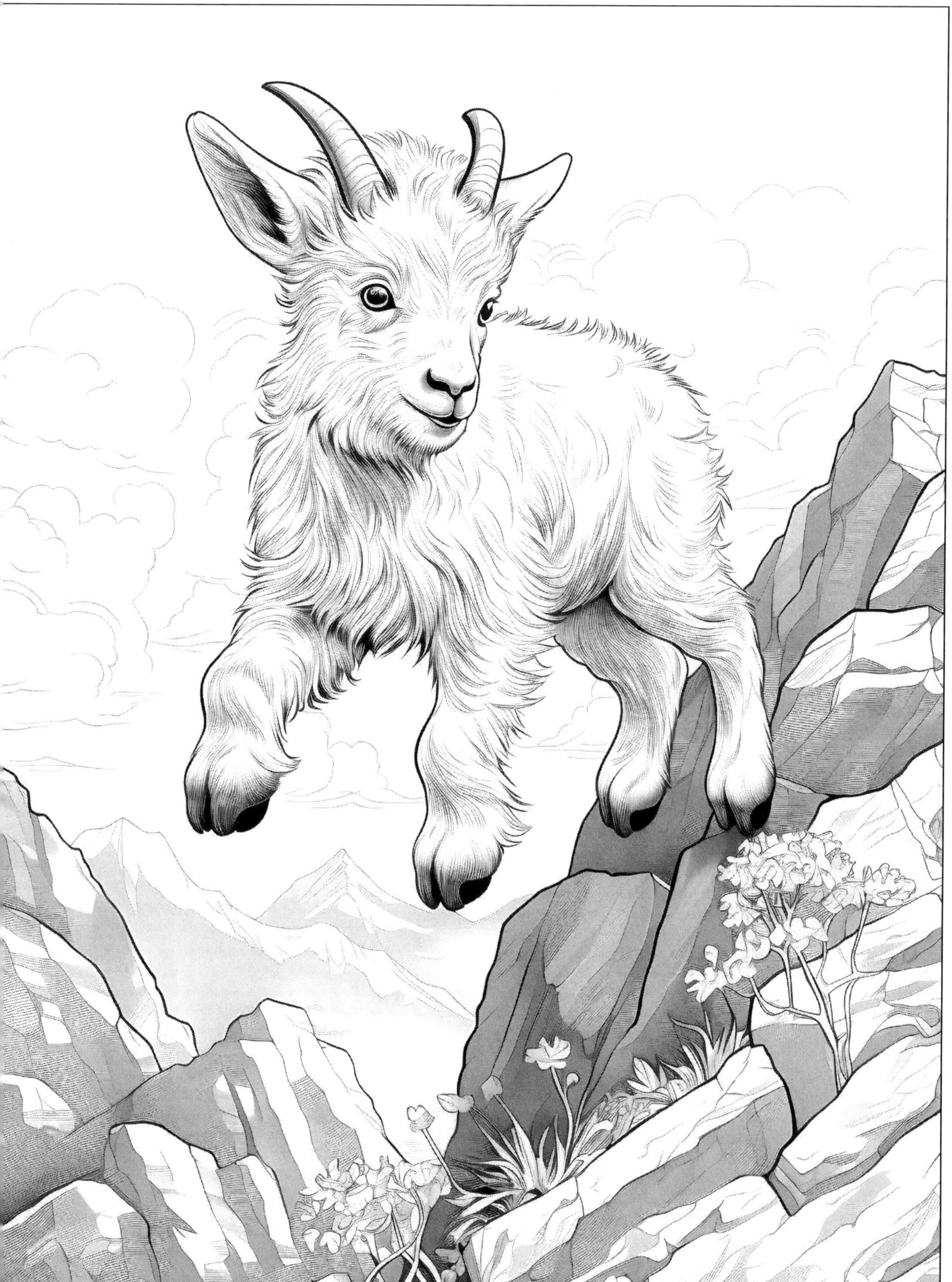

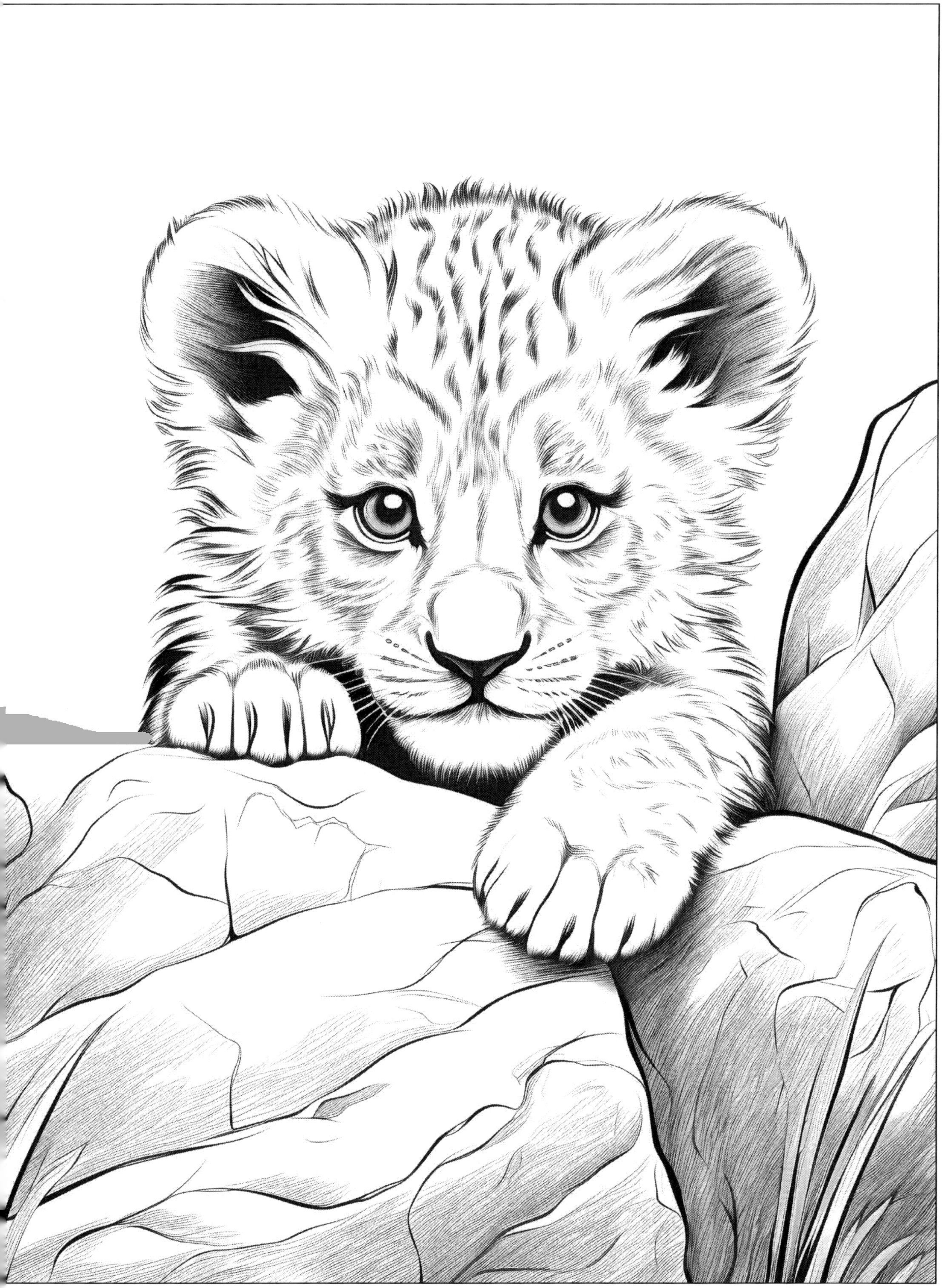

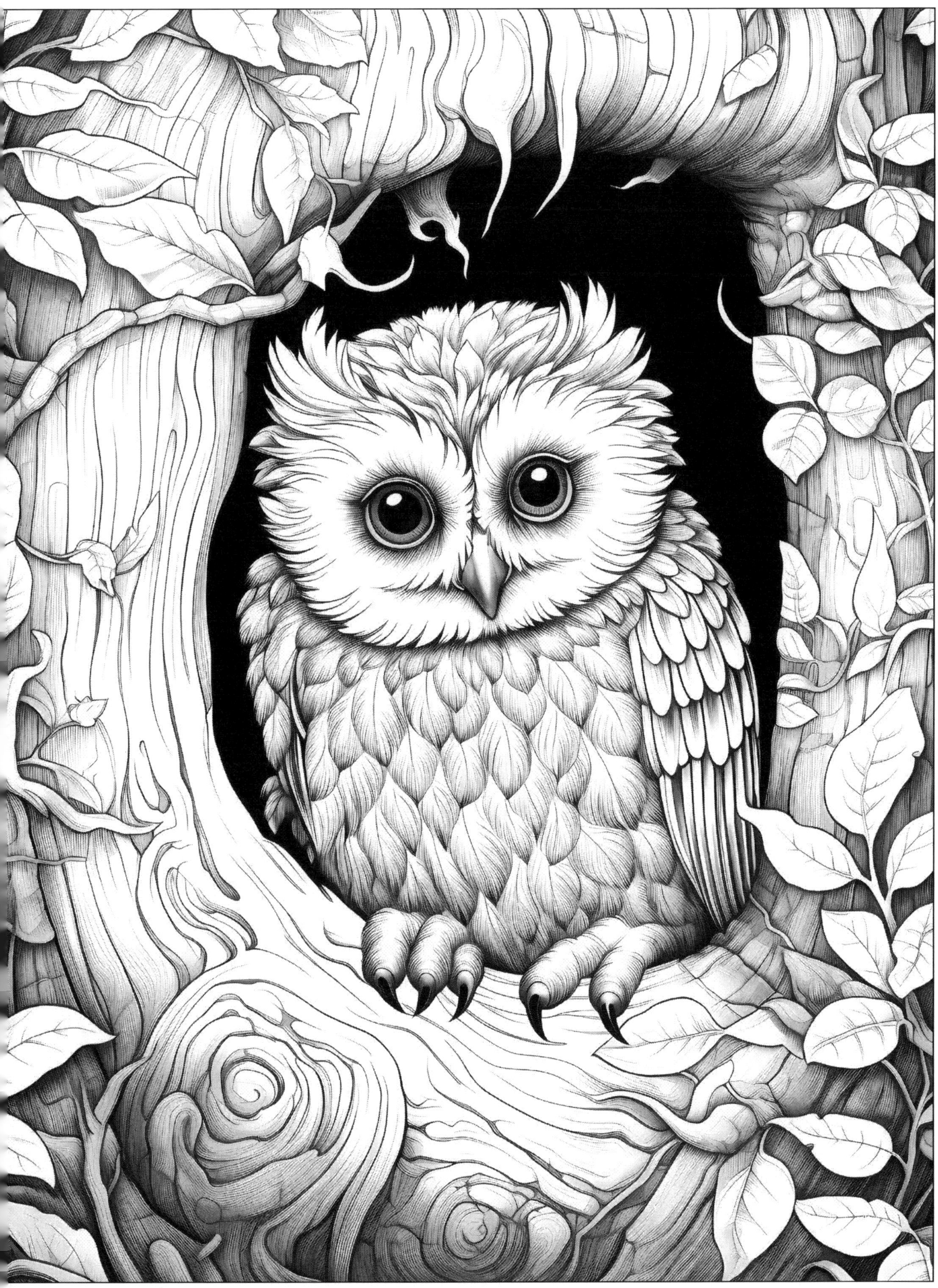

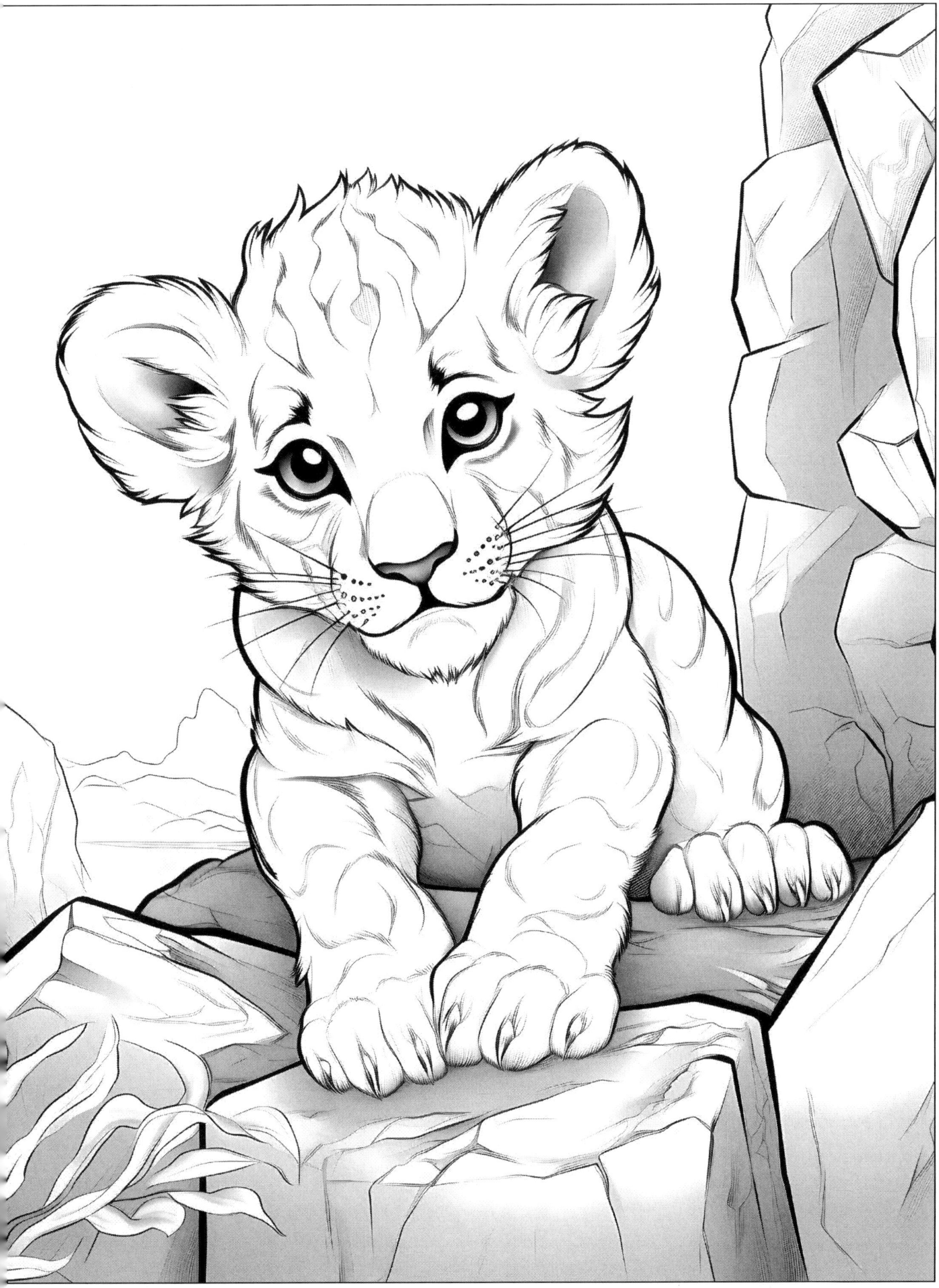

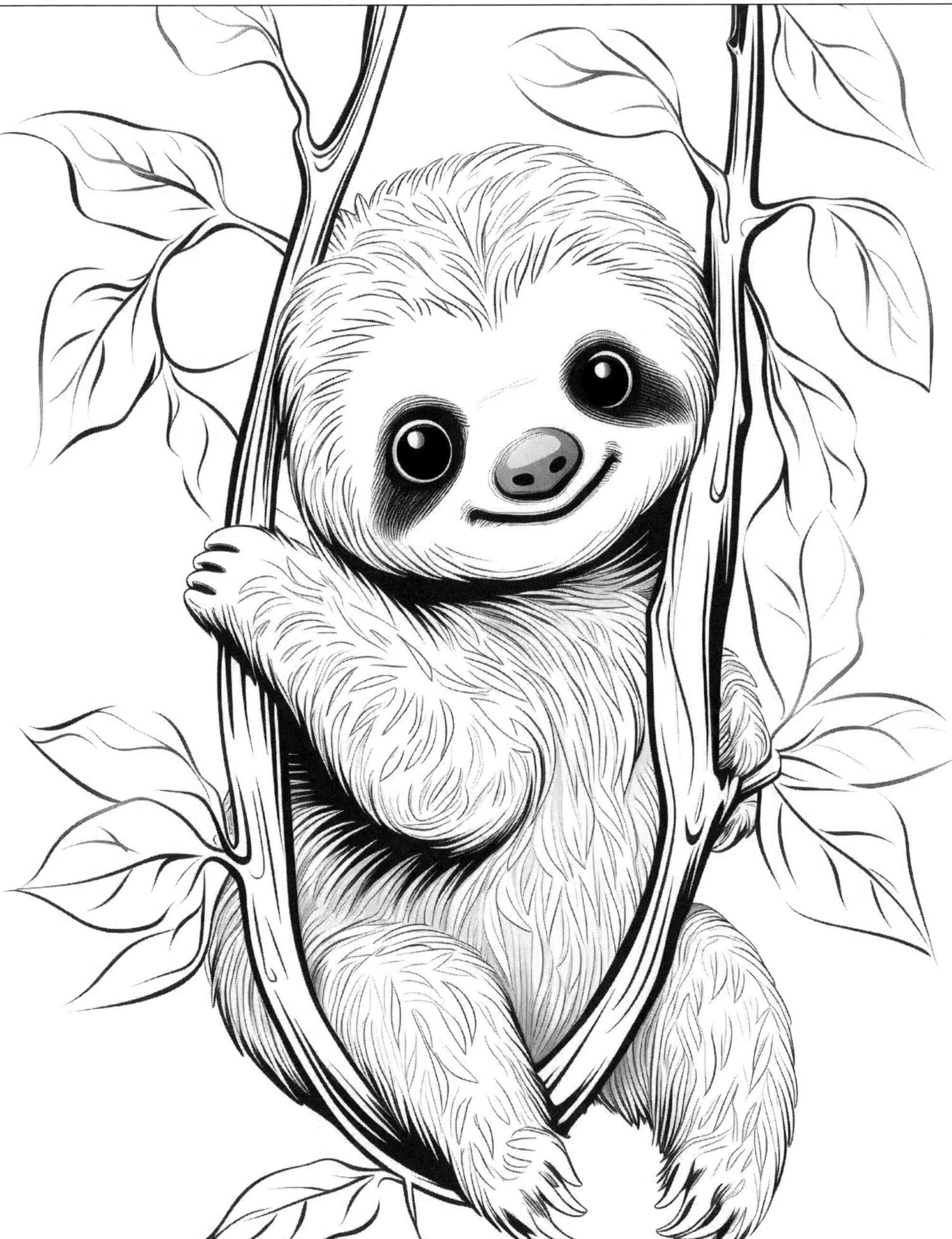

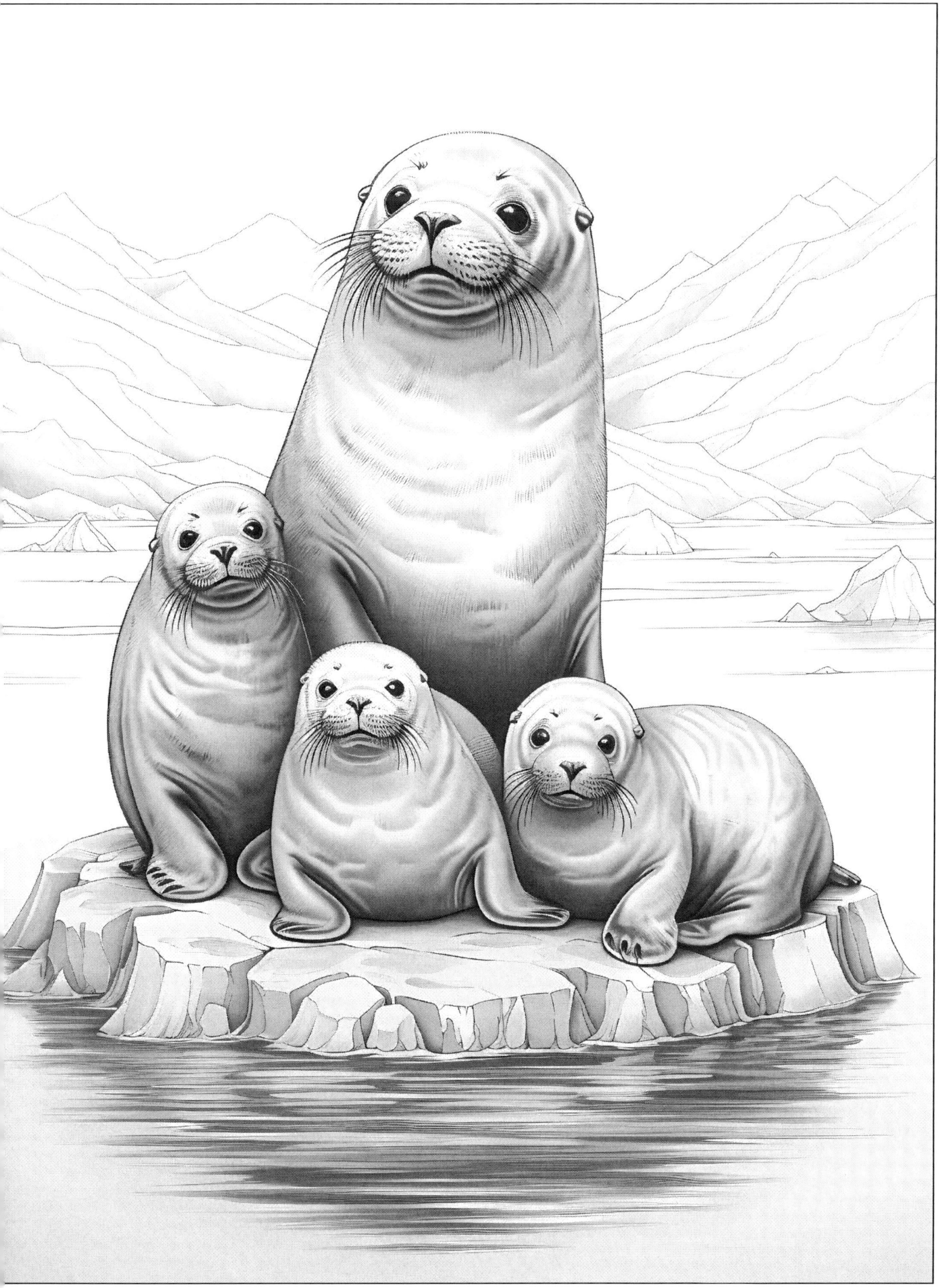

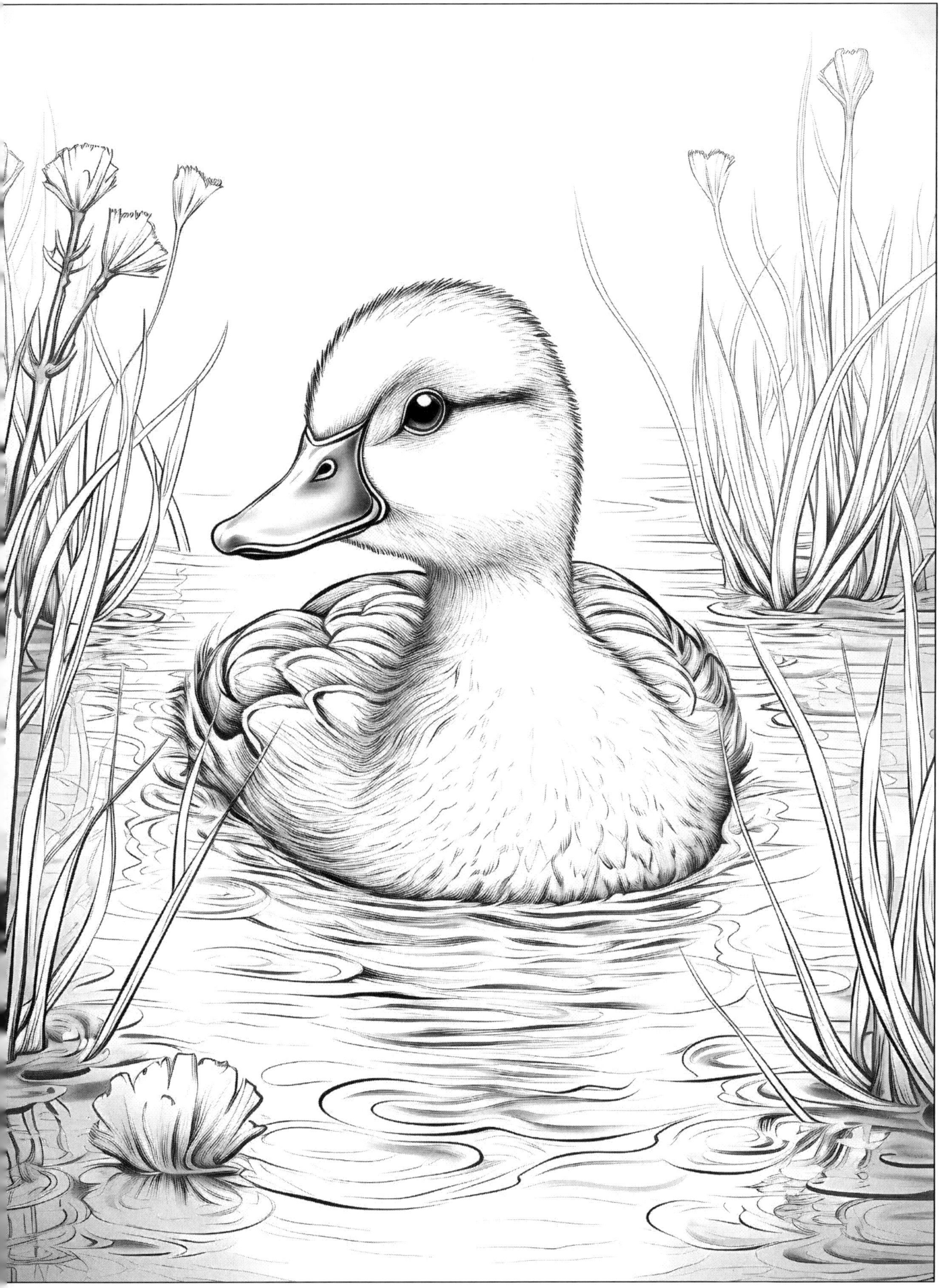

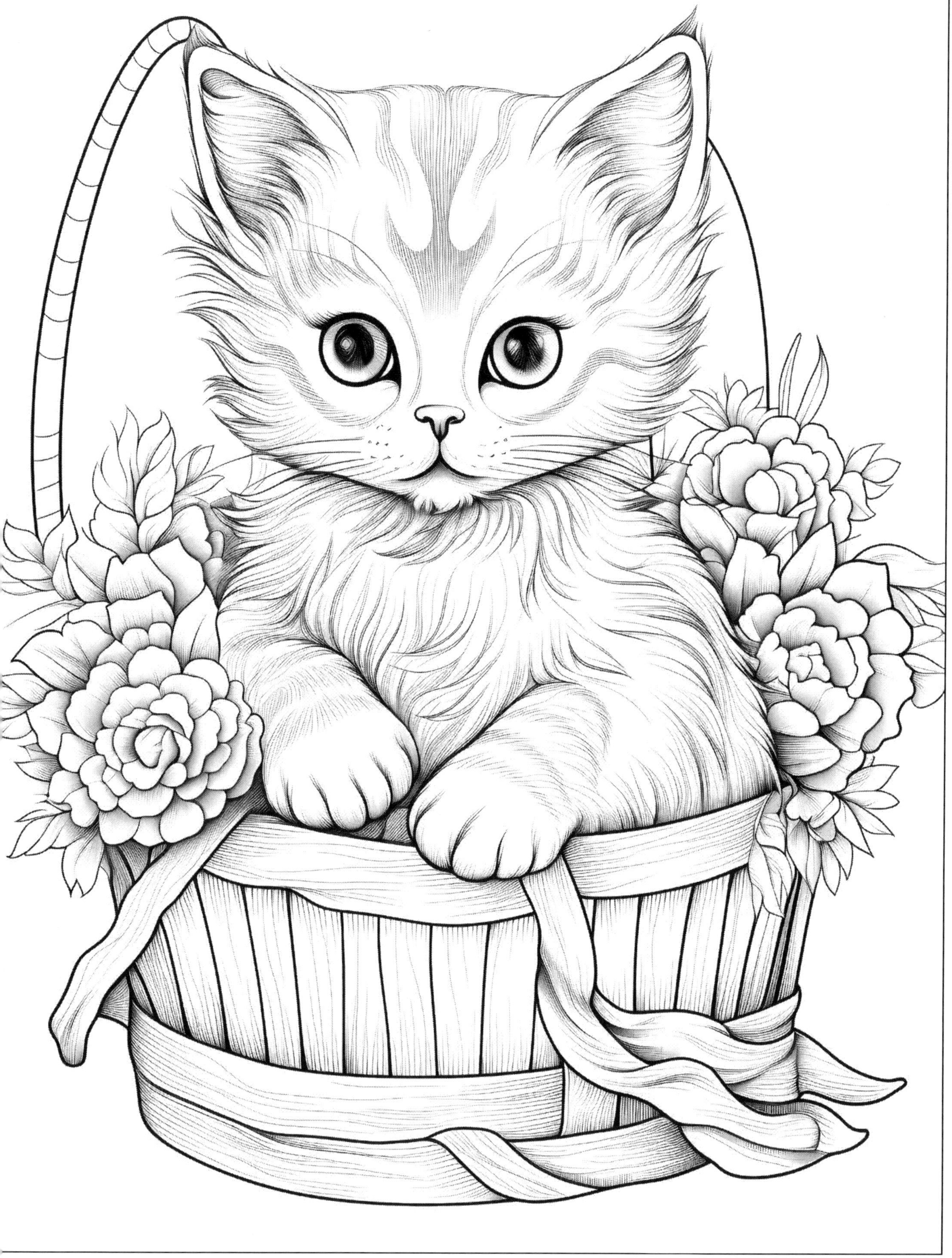

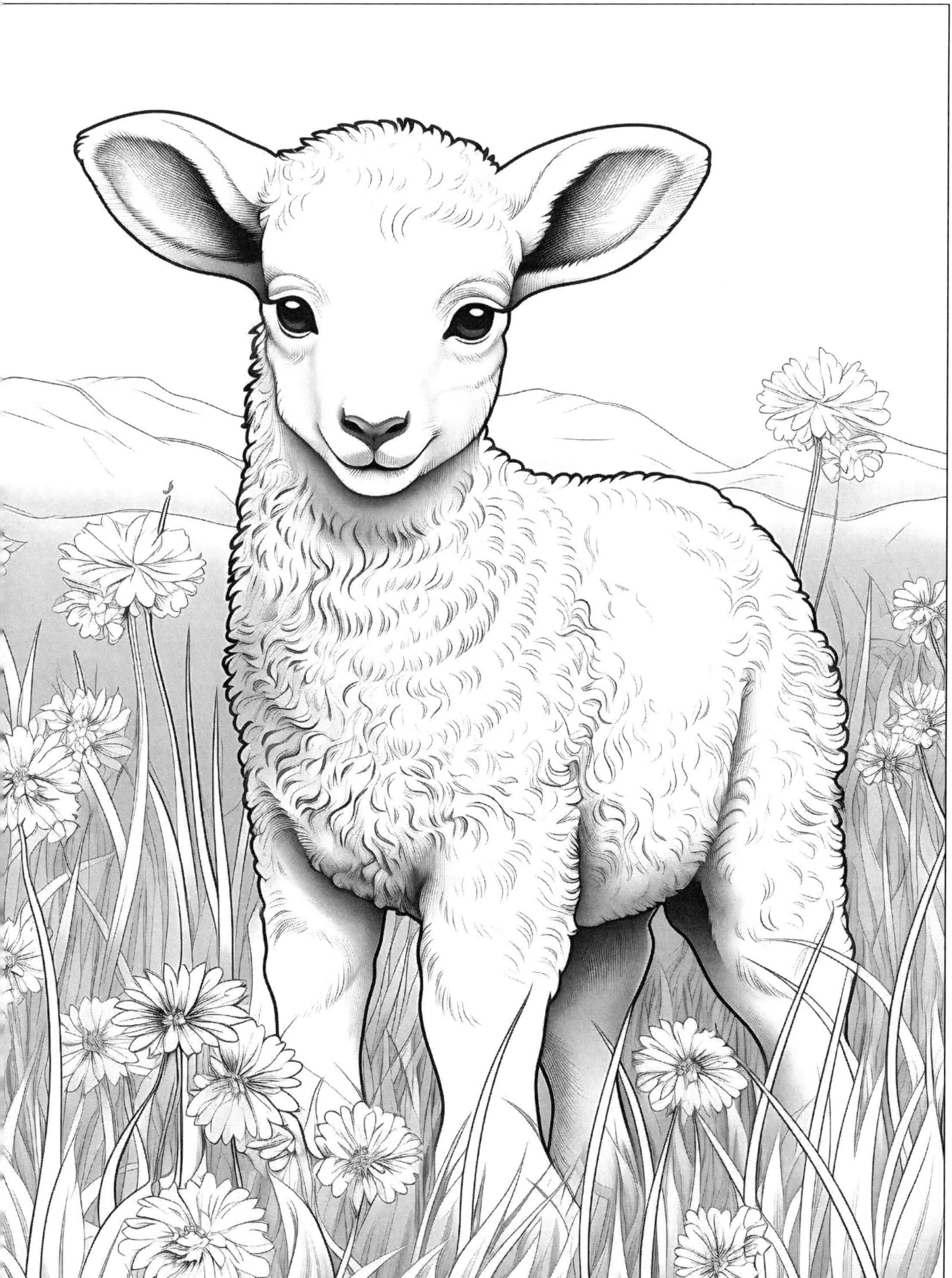

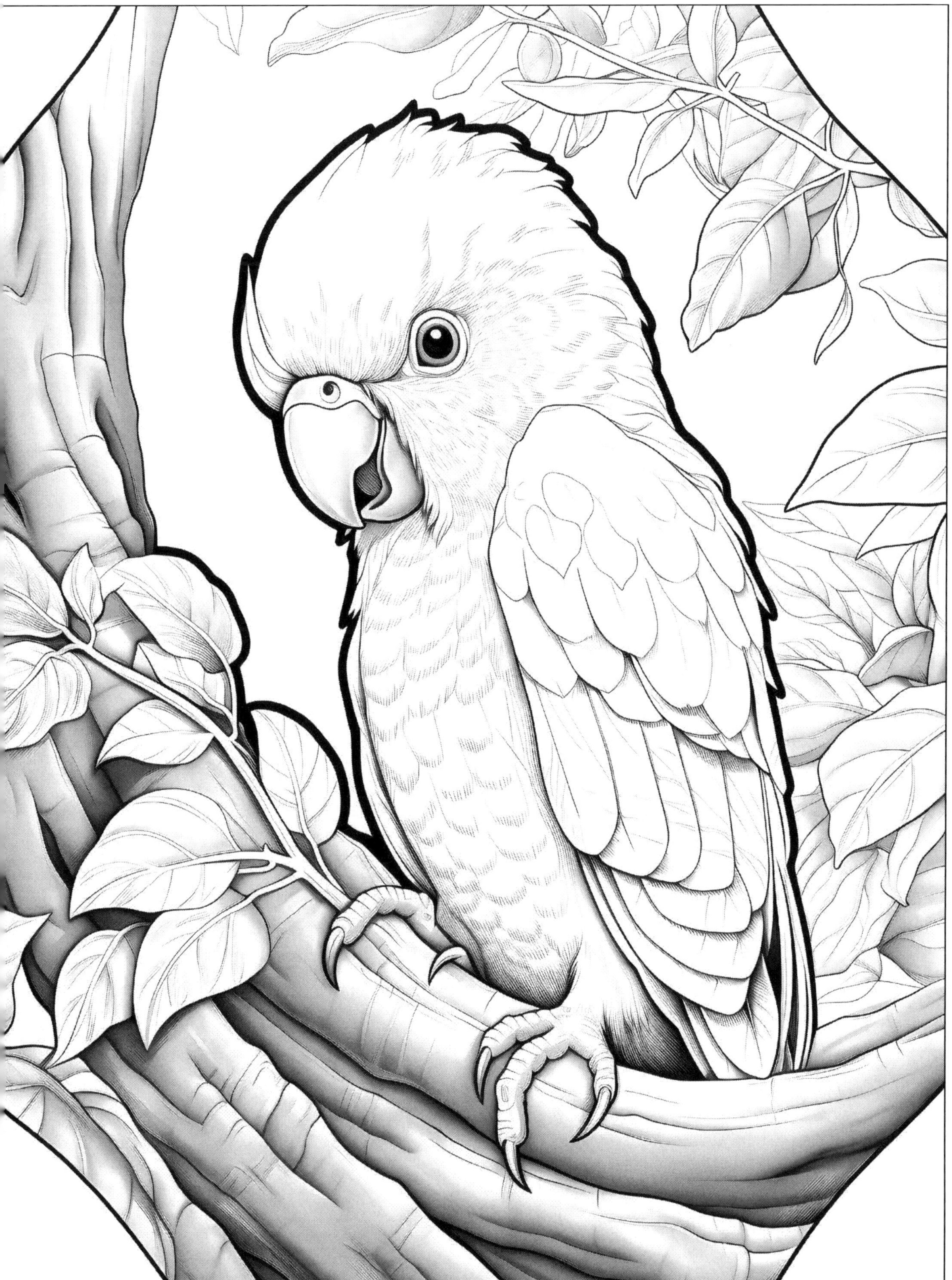

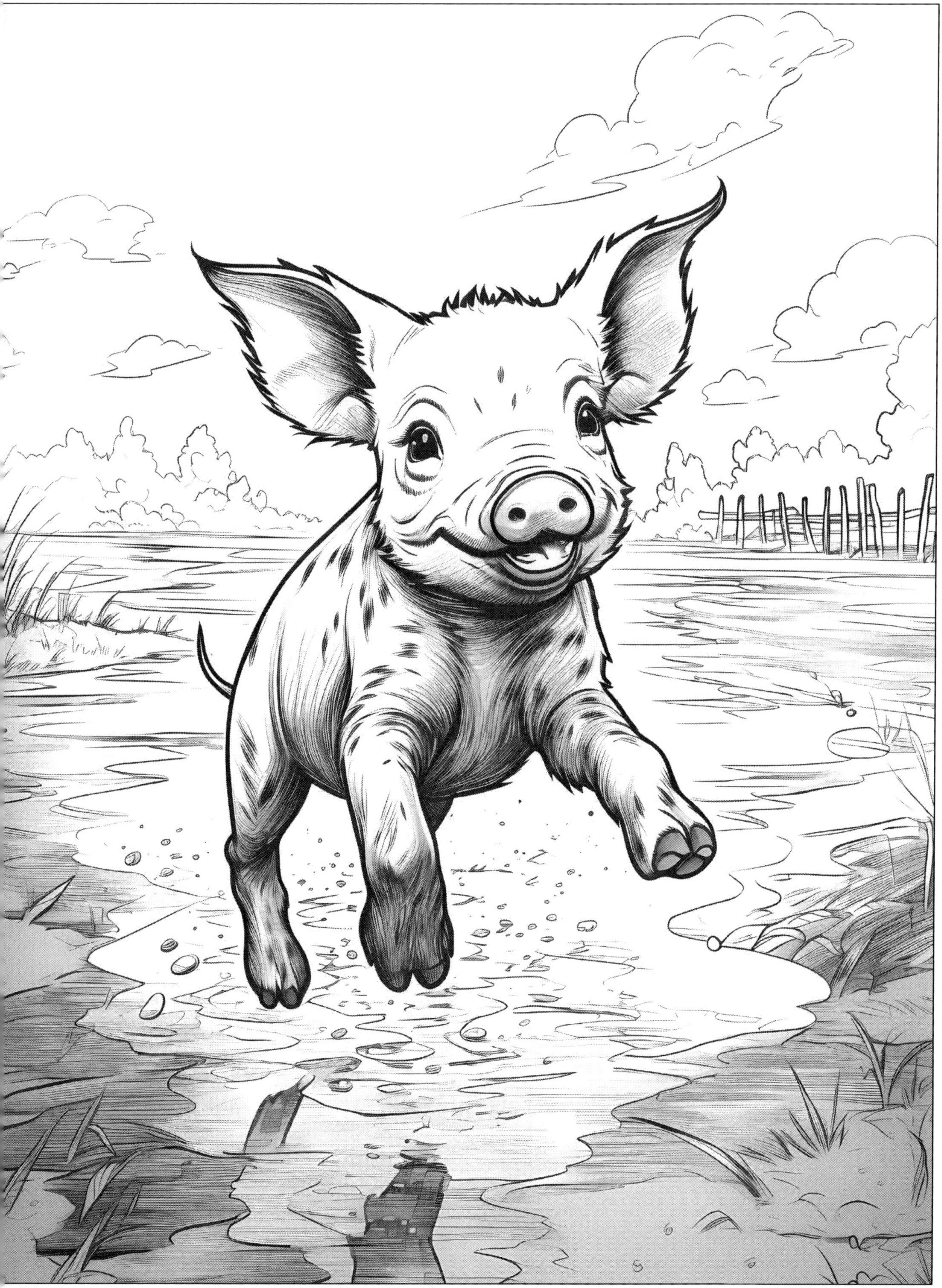

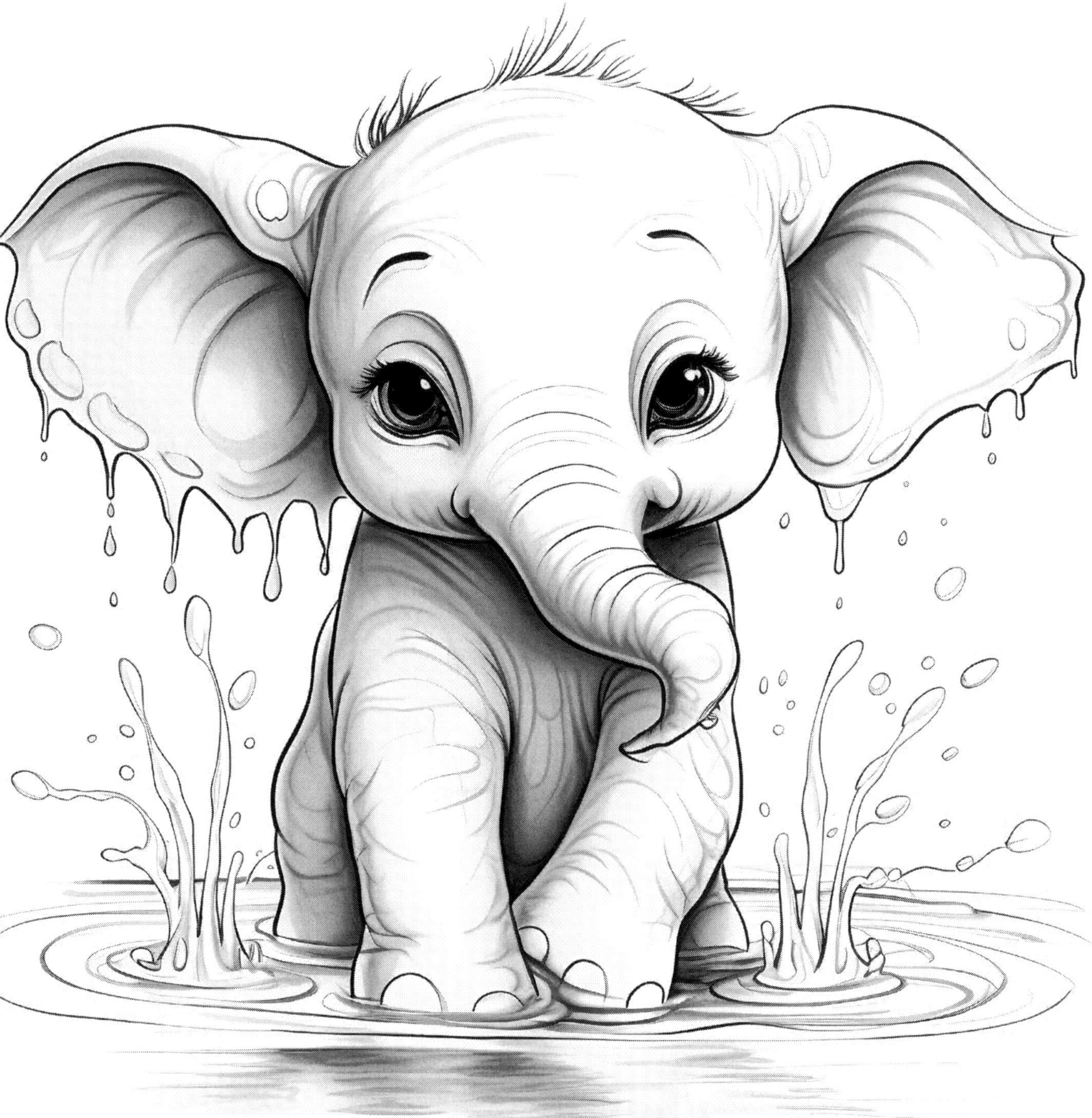

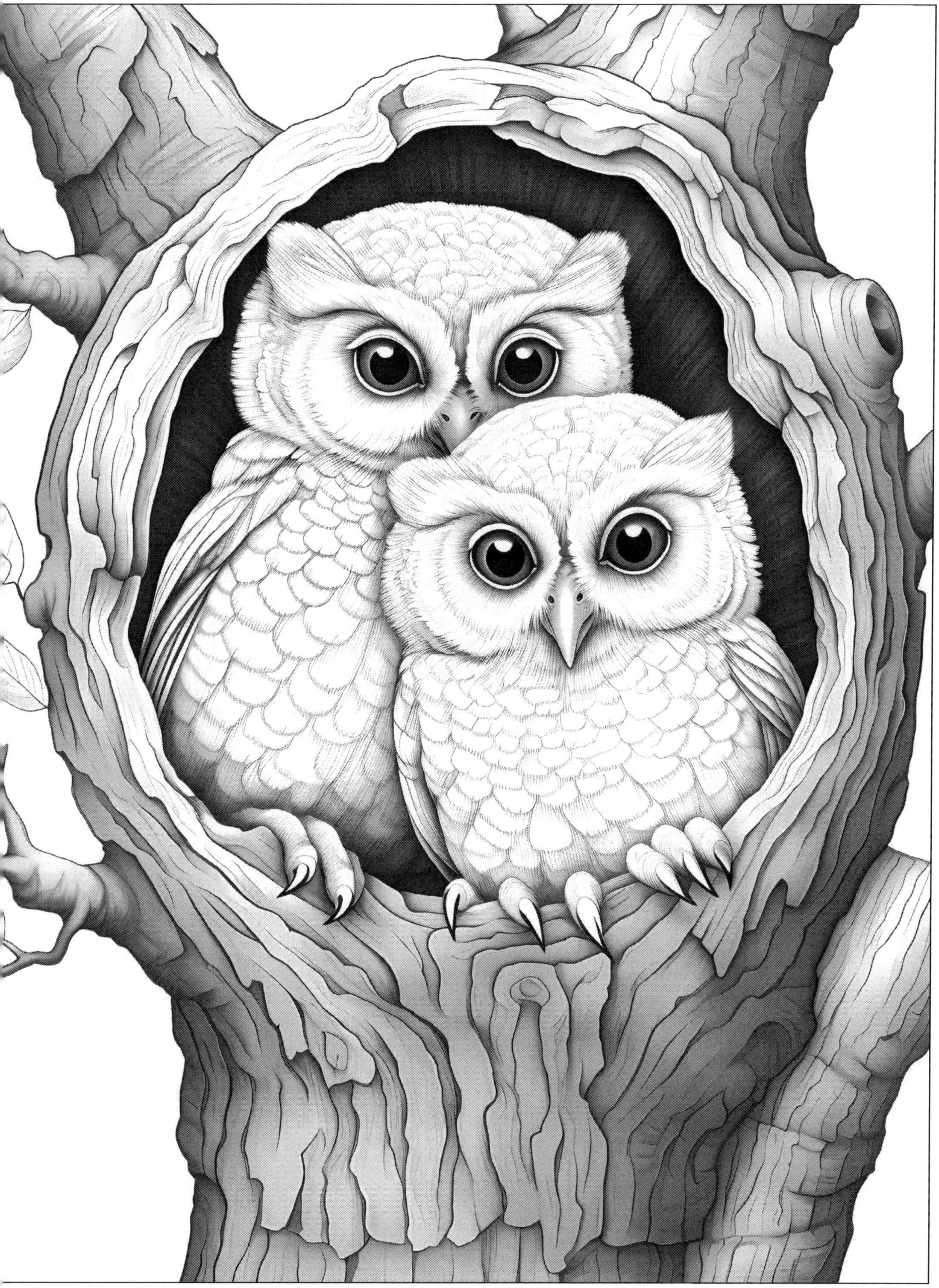

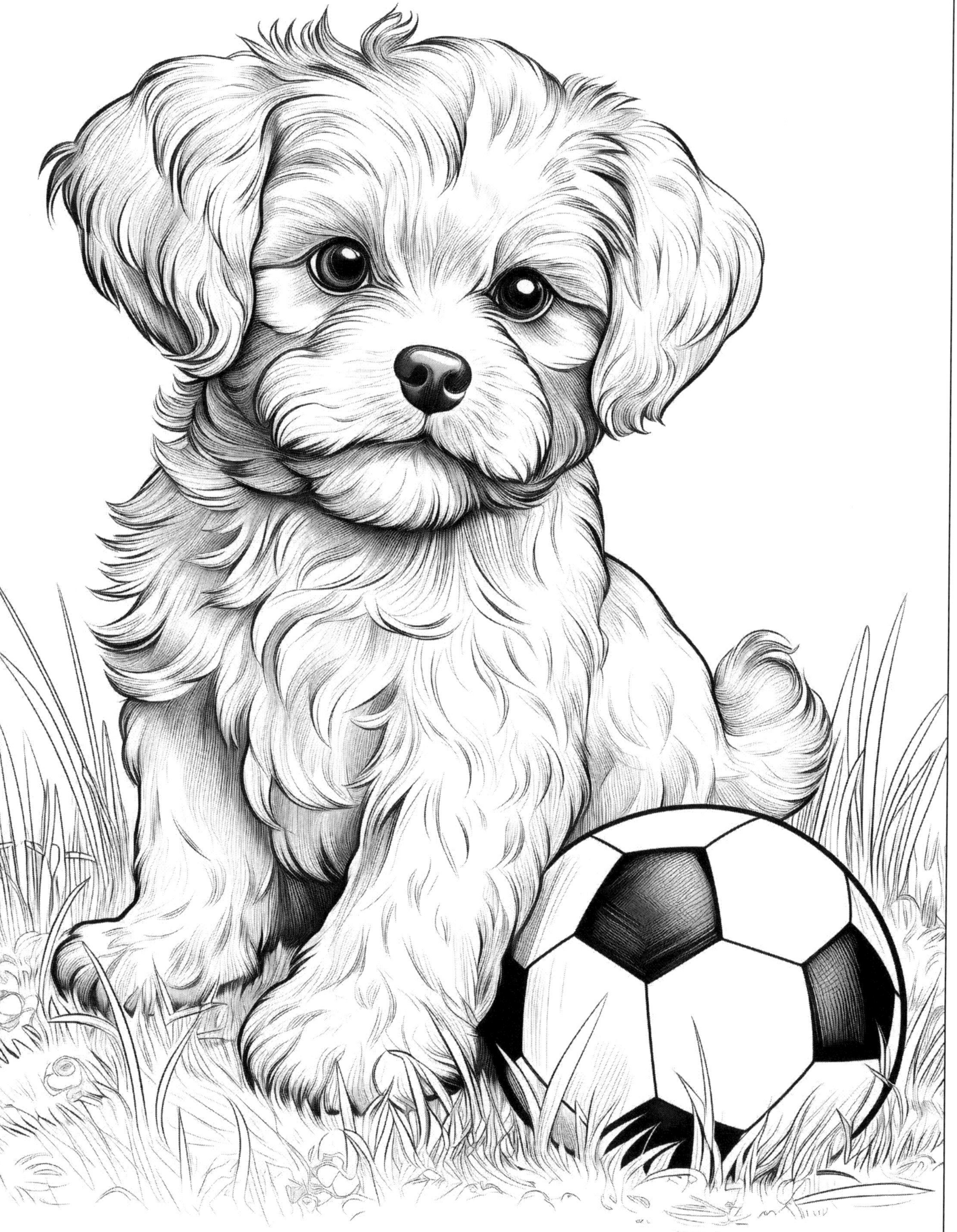

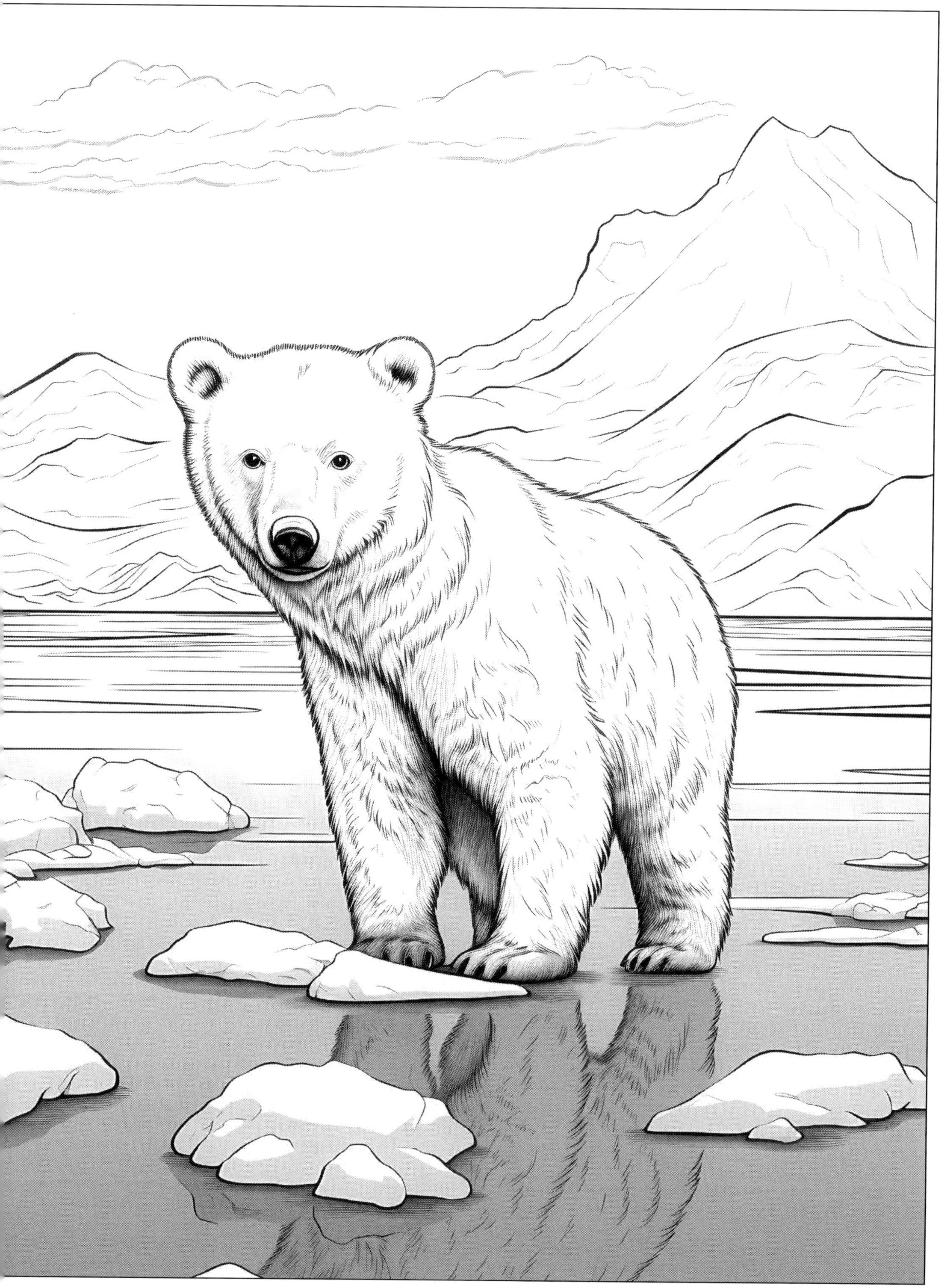

Made in the USA
Las Vegas, NV
06 December 2024

13447406R00059